RICHARD WAGNER

# THE LIFE OF
# RICHARD WAGNER

BY
DAVID FALKAYN

*WITH SEVEN ILLUSTRATIONS
FROM PHOTOGRAPHS*

**Fredonia Books
Amsterdam, The Netherlands**

The Life of Richard Wagner and the Wagnerian Drama

by
David Falkayn

ISBN: 1-58963-927-8

Copyright © 2002 by Fredonia Books

Reprinted from the 1915 edition

Fredonia Books
Amsterdam, The Netherlands
http://www.fredoniabooks.com

All rights reserved, including the right to reproduce this book, or portions thereof, in any form.

In order to make original editions of historical works available to scholars at an economical price, this facsimile of the original edition of 1915 is reproduced from the best available copy and has been digitally enhanced to improve legibility, but the text remains unaltered to retain historical authenticity.

## GENERAL NOTE

*Of all books perhaps the one best designed for training the mind and forming the character is "Plutarch." The lives of great men are object-lessons. They teach effort, devotion, industry, heroism and sacrifice.*

*Even one who confines his reading solely to biographies of thinkers, writers, inventors, poets of the spirit or poets of science, will in a short time have acquired an understanding of the whole History of Humanity.*

*And what novel or what drama could be compared to such a history? Accurate biographies record narratives which no romancer's imagination could hope to rival. Researches, sufferings, labors, triumphs, agonies and disasters, the defeats of destiny, glory, which is the "sunlight of the dead," illuminating the past, whether fortunate or tragic,—such is what the lives of Great Men reveal to us, or, if the phrase be allowed, paint for us in a series of fascinating and dramatic pictures.*

*This series of biographies is accordingly intended to form a sort of gallery, a museum of the great servants of Art, Science, Thought and Action.*

*On the mountain tops we breathe a purer and more vivifying air. And it is like ascending to a moral mountain top when we live, if only for a moment, with the dead who, in their lives did honour to mankind, and attain the level of those whose eyes now closed, once glowed like beacon-lights, leading humanity on its eternal march through night-time towards the light.*

# CONTENTS

## Part First

### THE LIFE OF RICHARD WAGNER

| CHAPTER | | PAGE |
|---|---|---|
| I | Richard Wagner's First Steps towards the Light.—From Poetry to the Theatre and to Music. — A Rebellious Pupil. — An Opera Staged in Ten Days.—The Trials of a Kapellmeister | 3 |
| II | The Calvary of an Artist.—From Hate to Love.—A New Art.—Waiting between Rays of Hope and Shadows of Despair.—The Revolutionist of Music | 37 |
| III | The Genesis of a Work of Art.—An Asylum: an Oasis in the Desert.—A Romantic Love.—From Real Life to the World of Thought and of Art | 57 |
| IV | Richard Wagner Greeted with Hisses.—The Splendor and Misery of an Artist.—Between Charybdis and Scylla.—On the Way to Success.—A King of Dreams and Mysteries | 76 |
| V | Peace and Meditation.—From Dream to Reality.—The Apotheosis of Richard Wagner | 110 |

## CONTENTS

### Part Second

## THE WAGNERIAN DRAMA

| CHAPTER | | PAGE |
|---|---|---|
| I | Some Principles of Wagnerian Art.—Poetry and Music.—From Opera to Drama | 135 |
| II | The Great Wagnerian Themes.—From Love to Sacrifice.—In the Realm of Dreams and Beauty | 147 |
| III | Epic and Lyric.—From Human Deities to Divine Humanity.—A Gospel in Music | 168 |
| IV | The Wagnerian Cult.—Those For and Those Against It.—The Initiated and the Profane.—Wagner in the Judgment of Posterity | 191 |

# ILLUSTRATIONS

RICHARD WAGNER . . . *Frontispiece*

FACING
PAGE

"RICHARD WAGNER, HIS FAMILY AND HIS PRINCIPAL INTERPRETERS AT BAYREUTH," *by* G. PAPPERITZ
*From left to right:* Siegfried and Frau Cosima Wagner, the painter Lenbach, the singer Scaria, the conductor F. Fischer, the celebrated singer Materna, Richard Wagner, the chief machinist at Bayreuth, Fr. Brandt, the conductors Hermann Levy and Hans Richter, the composer Liszt, the baritone Betz, the Countess Schleinitz, the Countess Usedom, the painter Joukowski . . . . . . . 16

WAGNER'S FAMILY
Frau Cosima Wagner and her son Siegfried are indefatigably devoted to the culte of the Master . . . . . . 48

WAGNER IN CARICATURE
*Above:* Caricature by Faustin (London *Figaro*, 1876), and by Gill (*Eclipse*, 1876). *Below:* Wagner as Première Danseuse, by Tiret-Bognet (1891); Wagner the Tetralogist, by Gill (1876) . . . . . . . 80

# ILLUSTRATIONS

**THE THEATRE AT BAYREUTH**   FACING PAGE
    Interior of the Theatre where the Pilgrims of Art commune in the Wagnerian Religion . 112

**THE PRINCIPAL INTERPRETERS OF WAGNER IN AMERICA**
    Mmes. Gadski, Destinn, Ober, Fornia. Messrs. Witherspoon, Slezak, Urlu and Kingston . 160

**RICHARD WAGNER'S MONUMENT AT BERLIN**
    This monument, erected in the Tiergarten in Berlin, by the sculptor Elberlein, is worthy of his universal and colossal glory . . . 208

# PART FIRST

# THE LIFE OF RICHARD WAGNER

# RICHARD WAGNER

## CHAPTER I

RICHARD WAGNER'S FIRST STEPS TOWARDS THE LIGHT—FROM POETRY TO THE THEATER AND TO MUSIC—A REBELLIOUS PUPIL—AN OPERA STAGED IN TEN DAYS — THE TRIALS OF A KAPELLMEISTER

ON the manuscript of one of Wagner's earliest operas, written in the days of poverty and anxiety, the following note occurs: *"Per aspera ad astra* (which may be rendered: By rough ways upward to the stars). God willed it so. Richard Wagner."

This formula admirably symbolizes the troubled and tumultuous life of this Titan of modern art, whose powerful genius created a world of new sensations and ideas by revolutionizing the æsthetics of music and the drama. It calls to mind at one and the same time his cruel trials, his ardent and sublime mysticism, his errors such as they were, and his marvelous ascension into radiant light.

The road that he traveled was full of black shadows and blinding brilliance, a Calvary before it became an apotheosis.

As was the case of Berlioz in France, before Wagner succeeded in winning the acclaim of the German nation and the world at large, he went through the atrocious torment of vain endeavor to obtain a hearing. He drained the cup of bitterness to the lees before his lofty inspiration at last triumphed and spread throughout all lands the superb, enchanting and torrential flood of his vast harmonies.

The one way to approach Richard Wagner is whole-heartedly, recognizing him as one of the boldest and noblest champions of the Dream and the Ideal. And no one can survey without amazement and something approaching reverence his remarkable destiny as musician, poet and dramatist.

Notwithstanding a sort of mystery which

seems to surround his prodigious career as an artist, it is possible for us to follow it almost without hesitation. And this is largely due to the fact that Wagner himself was profoundly, almost passionately anxious to make his contemporaries and posterity acquainted with his ideas and his life.

We can best initiate ourselves into these lofty ideas and into what we may call the Wagnerian religion, through the aid of Wagner himself, thanks to his important literary contributions, his *Memoirs*, his *Correspondence*, and the various other writings which bear the stamp of his immense personality.

Accordingly we shall rely largely upon Wagner himself in our attempt to understand and interpret him. Yet there are many other heralds of his fame, the majority of whom are as conscientious as they are well informed. For not only in Germany but in France as well Wagner has attracted a host of fervent enthusiasts. Indeed, it is astonishing to see how many writers have drawn their inspiration from the Wagnerian spring! Few men have shared with the author of *Tannhäuser,* the *Flying Dutchman* and the *Walkyrie,* the gift of attracting and retaining pilgrims of the ideal and the beautiful.

Undoubtedly, it was because he was at first misunderstood and even ridiculed, that he was afterwards all the more beloved and venerated. Undoubtedly, his legitimate glory profited by those earlier hostilities, and it was deemed necessary to avenge them by a devotion that was at times over partial and sterile. Yet fashion and snobbishness have been as powerless to harm him as was blind hostility. Vain clamors and excessive and sterile adulation alike subside necessarily with the passage of years. Yet such abatement takes nothing from the splendor and majesty of Richard Wagner, creator of the musical drama. It is no longer necessary to be fanatical in order to be able to admire him as he deserves and to continue a faithful worshiper at his shrine.

"My name is Wilhelm Richard Wagner, and

I was born at Leipzig on the 22d of May, 1813.

"My father was chief of police, and he died six months after my birth. My step-father, Ludwig Geyer, was an actor and painter; he was also the author of a few comedies; one of them, *The Massacre of the Innocents*, was successful. With him, our family removed to Dresden. It was his desire that I too should become a painter, but I had very little talent for drawing.

"My step-father also died prematurely, when I was only seven years of age. Shortly before he died, I had learned to play two pieces on the piano, *Üb' immer Treu und Redlichkeit* and the *Jungfernkranz*, which then had the advantage of being new. The night before he died, he had me play these two pieces in the room adjoining his own; and then I heard him say to my mother in a feeble voice:

"'Perhaps the boy has a talent for music!'

"The following morning, after his death, my mother came into the nursery and said to me,

'He was in hopes of making something of you.'

"I remember that for a long time afterwards, I clung to the idea that they were going to make something out of me."

Such is the beginning of the *Autobiographical Sketch,* from the French version by a musical critic of repute, M. J. G. Prud'homme, to whom we owe some valuable details regarding Wagner. But we need to supplement the above account with further information in regard to Wagner's family and the environment in which he passed his childhood and youth. Let us begin by casting a glance at his progenitors. They were of Saxon stock and belonged to a class that, although in modest circumstances, thirsted for culture; in fact, they were most of them organists or school teachers.

Wagner's grandfather, who had once made a serious study of theology, and his father, who was passionately fond of the theater, both led the peaceful life of government employees, the former as a post-office clerk, the latter, as we have already seen, as chief of police, at Leipzig.

Richard was Friedrich Wagner's ninth child. And although the family was far from prosperous, they were all deeply interested in art and learning. His mother, whose maiden name was Rosina Peetz, had many very estimable qualities. His father died on the 22d of November, 1813, a victim of the epidemic which broke out as an after consequence of the sanguinary battle of Leipzig.

Ludwig Geyer, his step-father, whom he always after held in grateful memory, had a number of real talents. He was an artist and more especially a portrait painter of some repute, an actor of ability, and furthermore he sang in the operas composed by Weber, who appreciated his fine voice and dramatic powers.

Adolf Wagner, Richard's uncle, was a scholar and man of letters, author of some remarkable translations and interesting comedies.

It was in August, 1814, that Geyer installed himself at Dresden; and from his childhood up, Richard lived among actors and attended rehearsals, even taking some small part in an occasional private performance. It was not long before his three sisters went upon the stage, and his brother, who was fourteen years older than Richard and was destined to be his chief protector after Geyer's death, renounced the study of medicine, in order in his turn to adopt the same career.

It is worth noting that Wagner, free and independent genius, was never subjected to that harsh intellectual discipline from which so many artists have had to suffer. He grew up in a congenial and pleasant atmosphere, in which every one had the right to consult his own tastes and devote his activity to them. Little Richard, for example, from the moment of his first intellectual awakening, conceived a passionate fondness for the theater. On this point Wagner's own autobiography gives conclusive testimony:

"From the date of my earliest childhood, the theater exercised a great influence over my imagination. I frequented it, not only as a child spectator, occupying a place in a box which mysteriously communicated with the stage, or as a habitué of the wings, admiring the extraordinary costumes and characteristic disguises to be seen there, but I also made my appearance as an actor. I had already seen performances of *The Orphan and the Murderer, The Two Galley Slaves,* and other somber dramas which filled me with terror and in which my step-father played the part of villain, when it came my turn to take part in certain comedies. In one piece that was produced on the occasion of the return of the King of Saxony from captivity,—*The Vineyard on the Banks of the Elbe,*—and set to music by the *kapellmeister*, Karl Maria von Weber, I played the part of an angel, and clad in tights, with wings on my back, posed in a tableau in a graceful attitude that was very difficult to take and to retain. I remember also receiving on this occasion a large sugar cookie, which, they told me, the king had had prepared especially for me. Lastly, I remember having had a speaking part of a few words in Kotzebue's play, *Hate and Repentance,* and that I made use at school of the pretext of a long scene to memorize as an excuse for not having done my lessons."

We next follow little Richard to Possendorf, near Dresden, to the home of a country clergyman, named Wetzel, who in the evenings related the adventures of Robinson Crusoe. He also read aloud a biography of Mozart, and newspaper articles about Greece.

A little later, we find young Wagner living with an uncle, a goldsmith, at the small and ancient town of Eisleben. He has recorded pleasant memories of a school conducted by a worthy man named Weiss, of Luther's house, and of the Market Place where he lived and where he had occasion to witness the performances of acrobats, who walked upon a tightrope stretched from tower to tower, all the way across the square. "For a long time afterwards," writes Richard Wagner, "I retained, as the result of this spectacle, a passionate interest in feats of this class. With the aid of a

## WAGNER'S FIRST STEPS

balancing pole, I myself succeeded in walking with some degree of skill upon a cord which I had stretched in the courtyard. Those days left me with a certain fondness for acrobatic exercises which I have not lost, even to this day" (*My Life*).

At eight years of age he entered the Kreuzschule, in Dresden. It was here that Weber's *Freischütz* filled him with enthusiasm, and he felt something akin to veneration every time that he saw the illustrious author of this opera, Karl Maria von Weber himself, pass by in the street. One of Wagner's teachers, who taught him Latin, began at this time to give him piano lessons. The boy had a strong repugnance for scales and exercises and put all his energy into picking out the overture to *Der Freischütz* after a fashion of his own. Horrified at his fingering, his master predicted that nothing could ever be made of him. As a matter of fact, Wagner never claimed to be a brilliant pianist. It is related that he contented himself with saying, at any joking reference to his lack of skill in playing, "I play better than Berlioz,"—which was by no means a difficult matter.

On the other hand, he seems to have received from boyhood up a solid course of instruction. His classical studies fired him with enthusiasm. At the age of eleven he was already grounded in Latin and Greek, and loved to brood over the great themes of mythology and ancient history. He began to write verse, and he wished to learn English in order to familiarize himself with Shakespeare, to whom he was strongly attracted. He straightway began the composition of a great dramatic work, *Leukald and Adelaide,* in which he undertook neither more nor less than a combination of *Hamlet* and *King Lear.*

"The plot," he writes, "was exceptionally magnificent; forty-two personages died during the action of the play, and towards the end I found myself under the necessity of bringing most of them back in the form of ghosts, for all my characters were dead before the beginning of the last act. This play occupied me for the space of two years."

We must not attach an exaggerated importance to the first stammerings of genius nor to the flattering accounts that are so apt to be given of such early manifestations. But it is at least curious to discover in young Richard Wagner this predominant taste for poetry and the drama and a predilection for vast subjects requiring a sovereign imagination and a most uncommon energy.

In 1847, the family returned to Leipzig, where Rosalie Wagner, who was then twenty-four years of age, had just secured an engagement at the municipal theater. It was at the Nikolaischule, in that city, that Richard lost his fondness for philological studies. Haunted as he was by dreams of the theater, it must be confessed that he proved to be a deplorable pupil. He hated what in later years he called the pedantry of schools and universities, and he did not hesitate to revolt against his teachers. Consequently the superintendent was obliged to make a serious complaint to his uncle, Adolf Wagner, in regard to the undisciplined lad.

Disgusted with school, Richard took his sister Ottilie into his confidence one day and read her his ambitious drama in the midst of a storm which, terrible as it was, was out-rivaled by his Goethe-like and Shakespearean scenes. His sister begged him to stop reading; but he continued imperturbably, and she submitted with touching resignation.

Mozart's *Requiem* and more especially the music of Beethoven came to him at this epoch as a revelation. He heard his elder sister, Rosalie, and more especially the second sister Clara playing the piano. "Clara," he writes, "possessed not only an expressive touch and a pronounced artistic feeling, but a voice that was extraordinarily beautiful and full of soul."

Young Wagner constantly heard discussions going on around him in regard to German opera and the Italian school. He himself took the side of German opera, partly because the

"RICHARD WAGNER, HIS FAMILY AND HIS PRINCIPAL INTERPRETERS AT BAYREUTH." By G. Papperitz.
*From left to right:* The painter Lenbach, Siegfried and Frau Cosima Wagner, the singer Scaria, the celebrated singer Materna, the conductor F. Fischer, Richard Wagner, the chief machinist at Bayreuth, Fr. Brandt, the composer Liszt, the conductors Hermann Levy and Hans Richter, the Countess Schleinitz, the baritone Betz, the Countess Usedom, the painter Joukowski

Italian tenor Sassaroli horrified him with "his high-pitched feminine voice and his noisy laughter, bursting out on all occasions."

From this time forth he held to the belief that the mission of music was to instill new life into the theater. He decided to write a score for his tragedy, and there seemed to him to be nothing unnatural in the project.

"I assumed without further thought that I was qualified to write the necessary music; but it seemed to me a good idea to begin by acquiring some knowledge of the principles of thorough-base. So, in order to lose as little time as possible, I borrowed Logier's *Method of Thorough-base* for a week and studied it zealously. But my efforts did not bear fruit as soon as I expected; the difficulties of the subject stimulated and delighted me; and then and there I determined to become a musician."

He became one very speedily, though at first with no very striking results. He planned an opera based upon the legend of *Faust,* and wrote a quartette and a sonata. At the age of sixteen he was author of a *Pastoral*. Weber and Beethoven had opened a path to him, and he boldly entered upon it.

His mother once more had him take lessons; but he rebelled against method. Anything in the form of discipline was hateful to him. Instead of drudging away at arid exercises, he preferred to compose overtures for the full orchestra, one of which was played at the Leipzig theater, on December 24th, 1830. Wagner's reminiscences regarding this maiden production are quite picturesque and well deserve to be reproduced:

"This overture was the culminating point of my extravagance. In order to render it easier to understand, I had persisted in writing it with three different inks, red for the string instruments, green for the wood, black for the brass. Beethoven's *Ninth Symphony* was to be reduced to the level of a Pleyel sonata, in comparison with this marvelously complicated *Overture*. . . . A kettle-drum, played *fortissimo* at regular intervals of four measures,

## WAGNER'S FIRST STEPS

turned the scales against me. The persistence of that drummer roused the audience, first to surprise, then to ill-concealed disapproval, and finally to an outburst of hilarity that filled me with consternation. That first performance of one of my own compositions has left a lasting memory."

Numerous anecdotes relating to Richard Wagner's youthful days have been given to the public by the pianist, Ferdinand Präger. Notwithstanding that, in the estimation of Mr. Chamberlain, their authenticity is extremely questionable, the following story at least ought to be cited:

"Richard Wagner's mother," writes Präger, "enjoyed a modest pension as widow of a government official. One day young Richard, being then fourteen or fifteen years old, was sent to collect the quarterly payment. On his way home, with the money in his pocket, he passed the door of a public gambling house. At that moment he had a sensation such as he had never before experienced. He felt as though the hazard of the die would serve him as an oracle of his destiny. The money did not belong to him, but none the less he entered, determined to tempt his fate. At first he was unlucky and lost all his stakes, until only a small sum remained. Yet he could not resist the fascinating temptation, but promised himself that this time he would stake his very life upon the turn of fortune. Fortunately for the world and for art, his luck changed. By a most unlooked-for run of luck, he won back not only the original sum but considerably more besides. He came out from the gambling house far richer than when he entered it.

" 'But,' I said to him, 'what would you have done if you had lost it all?'

" 'Good God!' he replied, 'before crossing the threshold of that house, I had made a firm resolve to throw myself into the river, if I lost, and on the contrary to believe in the greatness of my destiny if I won.'

"At the time that he told me this story, he was a man forty-three years of age, and I could not resist repeating my question: 'Would you really have done it?'

" 'I certainly should,' he answered, briefly and decidedly.

"The lad found himself incapable of hiding what he had done from his mother, but told her the whole story as soon as he returned home.

" 'Instead of scolding me,' he said, 'she threw her arms around my neck, kissed me tenderly and cried: "Your voluntary confession proves to me that you will never do such a wicked thing again." '

"Wagner told me this story while I was staying with him at Zurich in 1856. This was not the only occasion on which he defied destiny. He was always filled with an invincible faith in his mission, which sustained him through many a trial and at the same time drove him into audacious actions before which a graver mind would have recoiled."

It is a well known fact that throughout his life, and notably in a number of far echoing pamphlets, Wagner vented his animosity against the Jews, notwithstanding that his orchestra leader at Bayreuth and a number of his friends were of that race. His resentment in regard to Meyerbeer and Halévy, who at that time were on the top wave of popularity in France and who watched with very doubtful pleasure the rise of a rival star of such magnitude, would doubtless suffice to explain his anti-Semitism.

Präger however gives another version, the responsibility for which we will naturally once more leave to him. At all events, it is a picturesque story and at least contains some elements of truth, if only the vivacity of feeling, the feverish impetuosity of the young poet.

"Wagner," narrates Präger, "knew the Israelites from close proximity in his earliest years and shared all the prejudices of his fellow citizens in their regard. In Leipzig there was a whole quarter inhabited by Polish Jews. All the legends with which it is customary to brand the persecuted race were circulated about them.

# WAGNER'S FIRST STEPS

They were accused, among other things, of offering up children in sacrifice. When anyone wished to frighten a little boy in Leipzig, he would tell him, 'The Polish Jew is coming!' The scenes that followed were extremely brutal, and often a poor Jewish child would be chased through the streets by a gang of boys, cruelly beaten and rolled in the mud, regardless of his cries. It is strange that Wagner, who was always opposed to acts of violence and oppression, never took their part. The reason for his antipathy was partly æsthetic and partly personal resentment. He could not pardon the Jews for the vulgar accent with which they spoke German. It seemed to him that they degraded the language. On the other hand, their extravagant gesticulation irritated him. He insisted that 'They acted like galvanized corpses.'"

It would seem that a disappointment in love also had its share in this indelible aversion:

"Among the friends of his sister Louise was a young girl named Leah David, the daughter of a wealthy Hebrew family. When she made a round of calls, she often left her dog, a handsome Dane, at her friend's house. Throughout his life, Wagner was extremely fond of dogs. He soon became strongly attached to the handsome animal that served the young girl as companion and protector. But it was not long before he had formed a far warmer attachment for the young Jewess herself, who was just his own age, namely between fifteen and sixteen years old, and possessed that dazzling and ardent oriental beauty that is so frequently met with among the Polish Jews. She was the intimate friend of Louise Wagner, who shortly afterwards became the wife of the famous German publisher, Brockhaus. Leah David made a speedy conquest of Richard Wagner.

" 'Never before,' he said, 'had I encountered a young girl so richly attired and so beautiful. Never before had I been spoken to with such oriental profusion of caressing politeness. Surprised and dazzled, I experienced for the first time the indescribable emotions of first love.'

## WAGNER'S FIRST STEPS 25

"Wagner was invited to call at the house of Leah's father, Herr David, the luxury and splendor of which completed the mental bewilderment of the young man. Leah was the only daughter and had lost her mother. The enthusiastic young musician, deeply attached to the big Dane and madly in love with the young girl, obtained permission to continue his visits. He did not declare his passion, but contented himself with the sympathetic welcome that was extended to him. At this time young Wagner was slender, somewhat undersized and absorbed in his own dreams. He was treated by the David family more as a young boy than as a suitor. If Leah was not at home when he called, he would sit down at the piano, or else amuse himself playing with the dog, Iago. His calls became more frequent and his attachment assumed a tone of intimacy. The number of musical evenings multiplied rapidly. At one of them a young Dutchman was present, a nephew of Herr David. He was a pianist and had precisely that technical dexterity which

Wagner lacked. Flattering applause greeted his performance. But Wagner, being jealous, allowed himself to make an indiscreet remark. He claimed that the pianist lacked feeling. Whereupon he was begged to play in his turn. But his playing was so defective that it called forth ironical comments from the Dutchman and a general laugh from the rest of the company. Wagner then lost all control of himself. Wounded in his most intimate emotions in the presence of the young Jewess whom he loved so madly, he gave rein to the full impetuosity of his temperament and replied in such rude and violent language that a death-like silence followed on the part of Leah's guests. Then he flung himself brusquely out of the room, took up his hat, said farewell to the dog Iago, and swore to avenge himself. He waited for two days; then, not having received any communication, he returned to the scene of the quarrel. To his great indignation, the door was shut in his face. The following morning, he received a letter bearing Leah's hand-writ-

## WAGNER'S FIRST STEPS 27

ing. He opened it feverishly, and felt that he had received a mortal blow. Fräulein David announced her forthcoming marriage to the hated Dutchman, Herr Meyers. Richard Wagner and Leah David never met again.

"In concluding this story, Wagner said:

" 'This was my first disappointment in love and I felt that I could never forget it.'

"Then he added with characteristic impertinence:

" 'After all, I believe that I regretted the dog more than I did the young Jewess.' "

While a student at the University of Leipzig, Wagner became particularly interested in the political and social ideas which had been disseminated by the Revolution of July. At the same time, however, he realized the necessity of working seriously in order to acquire that knowledge of musical technique that would assure him a free expansion of his natural and original powers.

Providence, as he afterwards acknowledged, brought him in contact with the very man that the situation demanded: Theodore Weinlig, *cantor* at the Thomas-schule in Leipzig. At the end of six months he had mastered the difficulties of counterpoint.

"Now you have acquired your independence," his master told him.

After composing a new *Overture*, which had a more encouraging success at the Leipzig theater than his former effort, young Wagner applied himself to the production of a symphony, in which the influence of Mozart could be felt. The theater, however, still fascinated him. After composing a *Scena and Aria*, he wrote the libretto for *The Wedding*, but the subject of this opera, which, as a matter of fact, was far from agreeable, displeased one of his sisters, and in spite of a sextette, which Weinlig pronounced quite satisfactory, he renounced the task.

This brings us down to 1833. Wagner felt the need of securing some sort of salaried situation. He applied first to the theaters and before long obtained a chance. It was, to be

## WAGNER'S FIRST STEPS 29

sure, quite modest. The offer came through his brother Albert, actor and director at the theater in Wurzburg. Wagner's duties were to rehearse the choruses and soloists, and he was to receive in payment a monthly salary of ten guldens.

He remained there a year, and won a reputation for his activity. Meanwhile he was writing the music and verses for *The Fairies,* a romantic work based upon *The Serpent-Woman,* by Gozzi.

Armed with the score of this new opera, in which, notwithstanding his enthusiastic imitations of Beethoven and Weber, it was subsequently recognized that he had embodied the first important draught of a true Wagnerian lyric drama, the young man returned to Leipzig. He was filled with the most ambitious hopes. Encouraged by the friends who had proclaimed in the public press their interest in his earlier efforts, he counted upon the sympathy of the director of the Leipzig Theater and the support of his sister Rosalie. But the director, a disciple of Mendelssohn, was unfavorably disposed towards him.

Wagner was destined to meet with many another trial and reverses of every sort. But he gave himself up to the sheer joy of living, and does not seem to have been unreasonably discouraged by this first disappointment. The celebrated singer, Schroeder-Devrient, revealed to him the power that lies in dramatic intensity, and this again was a fruitful discovery, for it set him dreaming of combining faultless harmonies with emotion and spectacular grandeur. It was from this moment that Wagner began to realize to what an extent a singer may realize the ardent thought of the author.

Accordingly, in no wise discouraged, he profited by a pleasant summer excursion in Bohemia to draft a new opera entitled *Das Liebesverbot* (The Love-Veto), or *The Novice of Palermo*, based upon Shakespeare's *Measure for Measure*.

At this juncture (in 1834) he was appointed musical director, or leader of the orchestra, at the Magdeburg theater. Wagner made a success in his new line of duties, but the theater's financial affairs were going badly. At the moment when the company was about to be disbanded, he succeeded in having his *Liebesverbot* produced. This was in 1836. It was nothing short of a *tour de force,* and Wagner himself has related in a most amusing manner the history of this more or less sensational production:

"With more light-headedness than sober judgment," he writes, "I ventured to undertake to stage this opera, which contains some extremely difficult parts, within a space of ten days. I placed my trust in the prompter and in my own baton as leader of the orchestra. With all their efforts the singers had not succeeded in memorizing more than half of their parts. To all of us the performance was a sort of bad dream. It is impossible to convey any idea of it. And yet such parts as were even passably rendered received genuine applause."

Nevertheless, out of devotion to their leader,

the singers had labored day and night. The leading tenor sought to cloak his unpreparedness behind a bold presence and a swaggering manner. It should be added that the management had not found the means to have the librettos printed; consequently, notwithstanding the greatest good will on the part of the author, the performers and the audience, the whole production seemed as unreal as though enacted by so many musical ghosts, while the orchestra added to the general havoc its overwhelming crash of confused sounds.

After a fruitless journey to Berlin, Wagner, who was now beginning to feel the sharp pinch of adversity, settled at Königsberg where he obtained an appointment as conductor of an orchestra. It was there, on the 24th of November, 1836, that he married a young actress, Wilhelmine Planer, who was quite pretty and greatly admired. The marriage took place in spite of his family's opposition and all sorts of material difficulties.

Wagner freely admitted later on that this

union was as big a piece of folly as the untimely production of his opera had been.

"I was in love," he said, "and I married out of sheer blind obstinacy. I placed myself and others with me in the lamentable position of a household without resources, precipitated myself into a condition of poverty which has brought thousands upon thousands of others to their ruin."

The situation really was lamentable; there was no exaggeration in the terms he used. In 1837 the theater at Königsberg went bankrupt, as that of Magdeburg had done before. Wagner, now without resources, made matters worse by his extreme jealousy. His wife even thought of leaving him; while he on his part considered the question of divorce. But she could not make up her mind to a separation and accordingly accompanied him to Riga, where he once again secured a position as conductor.

Wagner performed his functions as musical director with alternate zeal and indifference.

from the month of August, 1837, until June, 1839. At times in his eagerness to achieve a sustained perfection down to the finest shadings, he wearied the members of the orchestra by long rehearsals, endlessly repeating the same movement; while at other times, although he chose a great diversity of works, ranging from Mozart and Glück to Bellini and Cherubini, he grew bitter and disheartened at the long delay of success and fame. At this time, it should be added, he gave little evidence of being the herald of a new and radical art. He realized the public demand for scenes portraying the pleasures and the passions of life; and he himself had a genuine fondness for Italian opera.

After *Rule Britannia* and the *Overture for Columbus*, he composed the libretto and the first two acts of *Rienzi*, based upon the novel by Bulwer Lytton. Staking all his hopes on this great tragic opera in five acts, he made up his mind to leave Riga. On the one hand his contract with the director of the theater was about to end and he was unpleasantly aware that he had competitors; while on the other hand, he was cherishing the project of going to Paris, in search of glory and gold.

This vagabond phase of Wagner's career, which had taken him all the way from the Rhine to the Duna, was destined, as Mr. Chamberlain has very justly pointed out, to be very far from sterile in its effects. In the course of it he had acquired some essential material for the future creation of his great musical dramas. Himself a German poet and playwright, he had learned to know and understand the profound aspirations of the German public.

This first period was one of struggles and gropings. Wagner was now in possession, if not of his full measure of genius, at least of his impelling desire to create. He understood the resources of the orchestra, and he thrilled with visions of the noblest emotions known to humanity. He had an immense pride, a dauntless, almost foolhardy courage, and a limitless desire to achieve beauty through harmony.

Where was he to find a field worthy of him and of his mighty activities, if not in Paris, the preëminent center of civilization, where the most illustrious reputations had been born and fostered?

We shall see that Wagner had not yet finished his struggles against ill fortune. But who can tell whether it was not essential to his genius that it should develop in the midst of suffering? And how could he have celebrated in *Tristan* and in *Parsifal* all the sorrows known to humanity if he had not been a hero himself, a victim of all the tragedies known to that great Drama called Life?

## CHAPTER II

THE CALVARY OF AN ARTIST—FROM HATE TO LOVE—A NEW ART—WAITING BETWEEN RAYS OF HOPE AND SHADOWS OF DESPAIR—THE REVOLUTIONIST OF MUSIC

IN September, 1839, Wagner arrived in Paris with his young wife, after a wearisome journey of three weeks and a half. They had embarked on a sailing vessel; and a raging tempest had compelled the captain to seek shelter in a small Norwegian port. By talking to the sailors, Wagner accumulated all sorts of information regarding the legend of the *Flying Dutchman*, which has been related by Heine, and which was destined to be the theme of his third opera, published in France under the title of *Le Vaisseau Fantôme*. His maritime adventures in a land wearing the aspect of dreams and nightmares must have greatly helped him to achieve the exact and picturesque color of his work.

He spent a week in London and a month at Boulogne-sur-Mer, where he made the useful acquaintance of Meyerbeer.

Without further introductions, without resources, and with little acquaintance with the French language and customs, but full of hope and energy, Wagner installed himself in Paris, with his wife and Newfoundland dog, in a furnished house on the Rue de la Tonnellerie, near the *Halles*.

An introduction from Meyerbeer, at that time all powerful, brought him into relations with Anthenor Jolly, director of the Renaissance Theater, who accepted his *Liebesverbot*. A vaudeville writer, Dumersan, who also had a reputation as a numismatist, was commissioned to adapt the work to the requirements of the French public.

Overjoyed and counting upon an early success, Wagner moved into a more comfortable apartment, No. 25, Rue du Helder. But ill luck pursued him: the theater went bankrupt! In France, just as formerly in Germany, he met with the same identical reverse. This time it was a veritable disaster. He passed through atrocious hours of chagrin, despair and ruinous destitution. Apropos of his short story, *A German Musician in Paris*, he wrote:

"I myself came very near dying of hunger in Paris, like the hero of my story. My purpose, by the way, in writing it, was to utter a cry of revolt against the conditions of art and artists of our epoch."

It would be impossible to paint in colors sufficiently somber the three years of lamentable distress that Wagner passed in Paris. He was forced to squander his energies on all sorts of unworthy tasks in order not to starve to death, grinding out articles for the reviews, and more especially making arrangements for various instruments, including the trombone, of the popular melodies of the hour, the most distinctive pieces by Donizetti and Halévy.

Consequently, it is easy to conceive his resentiment, not only against these composers who had already "arrived," but against Paris itself, which he had failed to take by conquest, and in which he had known, to use his own expression, "the black misery of long nights of suspense and anguish." It was all in vain that his young wife performed prodigies of economy and maintained an indomitable courage; it was equally in vain that his rare moments of leisure gave him a chance to chat pleasantly with a few friends, such as the painter Kietz and the librarian Anders.

Nevertheless, despite the bitterness of defeat and the disheartening melancholy of vanished hopes and repeated failures, Wagner continued to work. He composed romances, such as *The Two Grenadiers,* he wrote an *Overture to Faust* and an *Overture to Columbus*. The latter, by the way, was the only work by Wagner produced in Paris during this period (February, 1841, at the Salle Herz).

The doors of the Opéra remained implacably closed against this foreign composer. He had now finished *Rienzi;* and being finally convinced of the impossibility of succeeding in Paris, he decided to try his luck in Dresden.

The winter of 1841 was one of the most critical periods of his whole restless existence. He found small consolation in listening to Beethoven's *Symphonies* at the Conservatoire, in selling the manuscript of his *Flying Dutchman* for five hundred francs, in studying the luxurious stage settings of the great Paris theaters, or even in pouring out his pent-up bitterness and rancor in articles for the *Gazette Musicale* and in literary problems of a morbid humor.

The reason why this lugubrious period must be regarded as important in the development of Wagner's real genius is as follows: side by side with his bitter revolt against the bad taste of the public and the vulgar sensuality of the fashionable composers, was born his determination to be a great revolutionist in the domain of musical and theatric art. His hatred of silliness and vulgarity, his disgust at all the humiliations inflicted upon his pride were accompanied by a love of beauty amounting to a magnificent religion.

He issued from all his defeats more exalted, and consequently, stronger than before. Hence came a tenderness and a fervor that added much to the loftiness of his inspiration. In this respect Wagner has admirably analyzed himself in the following terms:

"I wish to speak here of music," he wrote in *A Communication to My Friends*, "as the good angel that assured my salvation as an artist. I owe it to music that I became an artist, beginning with the day when, in a spirit of revolt, I rose up in protest, with a growing clearness of purpose, against the existing conditions under which art had to manifest itself to the public. This feeling of rebellion was not born from a point of view external to art, like that of our critics, for example, or of our mathematicians of current politics, enemies of art and socialistic calculators; on the contrary, my revolutionary instinct served to awaken

## CALVARY OF AN ARTIST 43

in my heart an inspiration, the faculty of creating a work of art,—and this I owed to music and to nothing else."

And Wagner added, "For my own part I cannot conceive of the spirit of music apart from love. It was love and not hate or envy that made me a rebel; and that is why I became an artist and not a critic."

It was in this state of mind of mingled pleasure and pain that Wagner installed himself at Meudon, in the spring of 1841. There he resumed, though not without some misgivings, his interrupted work upon the *Flying Dutchman*. But after finishing the chorus of sailors and the song of the spinners, he felt sure of himself, and in a short time the opera was completed. This work in a certain way bears the material traces of the composer's struggle against want, for at the end of the second act the manuscript of the *Flying Dutchman* contains this painful indication: "Tomorrow, must have more money," and at the end of the third we read: "Meudon, August

22d, 1841. Written in poverty and torments."

Seized with nostalgia for his native land, that he aggravated still further by brooding over the popular German legend of *Tannhäuser,* Wagner impatiently waited for favorable news. *Rienzi,* which had been accepted by the Dresden Theater, was at last to be put into rehearsal. Meanwhile, the *Flying Dutchman* had found favor at Berlin, thanks to the mediation of Meyerbeer.

Wagner now dreamed of nothing else than his return to Germany. In order to earn the cost of the journey he resumed almost light-heartedly the tasks of a musical hack and proceeded to raise the necessary funds by arranging the scores of Halévy's operas for the piano. Henceforward, however, he was to be relieved from the necessity of any such wretched drudgery.

On April 7th, 1842, he left Paris, the vast and tumultuous City of Light, in which he had suffered so keenly from his obscurity, and towards which, in spite of his anger and bitterness, he afterwards looked back wistfully, with a secret desire to see his German achievements and reputation further augmented by the applause of France. When he reached the Rhine he shed tears and swore fidelity to the fatherland. In default of Paris and of France, which were destined later on to recognize his splendid genius, he set forth to conquer Germany by drawing his inspiration from her legends and most deep-rooted traditions.

Wagner's sojourn in Dresden, where he remained seven years, is a characteristic and decisive epoch in his life. He there accomplished his definitive rupture with traditional opera, and it was there that he acquired a clear and direct understanding of his temperament, his work and his mission.

On October 20th, 1842, *Rienzi* was produced at the Dresden Opera House, and proved to be not only a success but a veritable triumph. Wagner became famous in a single day, even though he was none too well understood. His fame was not yet the sort that he deserved, but then in *Rienzi* he had not yet produced a "Wagnerian" opera.

This success brought about a radical alteration in Richard Wagner's career. In order to reach a better interpretation of the significance of such an event in a life which, to borrow his own terms, had hitherto been "disjointed and over-burdened," let us see what he himself has said:

"After a most painful struggle, after hard conflicts, suffering and privation, in the midst of the agitation and the indifference of Paris, I found myself all of a sudden in an attentive world, full of encouragement and consideration. . . . How natural it was that I should have allowed myself to be rocked in the cradle of these illusions, from which I must soon be awakened, the victim of a cruel experience! If anything was capable of deceiving me as to my true position at that time, it was the uncommon success achieved in Dresden by the performance of my *Rienzi*. I, a solitary man, friendless and without a country, suddenly found myself beloved, admired and flattered by a multitude of followers. In view of the established conditions of life, this success ought to have given my career a lasting foundation of artistic and bourgeois prosperity. To the surprise of the general public, I was appointed *Kapellmeister* to the court of Saxony."

This unexpected appointment, due partly to the simultaneous death of two incumbents, and partly to the activity displayed by Wagner in training the orchestra at the time his opera was produced, did him almost as much harm as good. To be sure, these functions which he performed from 1843 to 1849, gave him great authority as well as an annual revenue of fifteen hundred thalers, or a little more than eleven hundred dollars. But Wagner had the legitimate ambition to develop his new conception for the benefit of Saxon and German art, and his apostleship was destined to encounter the opposition of tradition, incomprehension, jealousy and even hatred.

*The Flying Dutchman,* also performed at

Dresden, had meanwhile achieved a success comparable to that of *Rienzi*, notwithstanding its innovations in technique. But before long the critics reconsidered their verdict; and from this moment the campaign against Wagner began, and this splendid and vital creator had need to summon up all his mighty will power, all his colossal energy, in order to hold his own against the adversaries of an art that was at once human and divine.

While *The Flying Dutchman* was announced for production at Berlin, Riga and Cassel, its performance was stopped in Dresden after the fourth occasion. In the king's Intendant, Baron von Luttichau, Wagner had found, if not an open enemy, at least a man who had small intention of abandoning routine and sacrificing the customary pleasures of the court and the general public, to the idealism of a revolutionary artist, and to his devout worship of the beautiful.

Now, as V. H. Lichtenberger, the author of

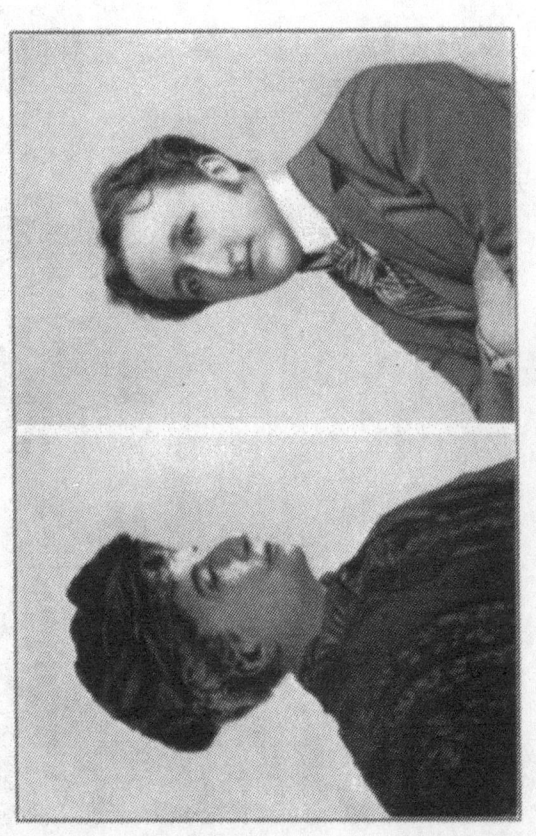

WAGNER'S FAMILY

Frau Cosima Wagner and her son Siegfried are indefatigably devoted to the cult of the Master

some important studies upon Wagner, has done well to remind us, the Dresden Opera House offered an ambitious artist exceptional chances of success. The theater itself, the orchestra, the chorus, the marvelous talent of Schröder-Devrient, whose gifted nature was so splendidly fitted for interpreting a noble genius, the glorious voice of the tenor Tichatschek, the financial resources at command, all united in enabling him to perform an important service to art, and base his productions on the stable foundations of his own fervid inspiration and his vast and profound experience of music and the theater.

Accordingly, we find him interpreting, with all the enthusiastic respect due to such masters as Mozart and Glück, *Armida* and *Iphigenia at Aulis,* and initiating Dresden into the splendors of Beethoven's *Ninth Sympathy.*

Meanwhile, during the year 1844, after finishing the *Love Feast of the Apostles,* he expressed his passionate admiration for the author of *Der Freischütz* by composing the funeral music on the occasion of the transfer of Weber's ashes to Dresden.

Wagner had now surrendered himself wholly to his religion of art, and he henceforth pursued his task of human and social regeneration with a sort of mystical fanaticism. *Tannhäuser*, the first performance of which he conducted on October 19th, 1845, was the fruit of prolonged meditation and the first great manifestation of Wagnerian art. He was destined to bring his art to a loftier and more sustained perfection. But he had now found himself, he had acquired his characteristic manner, ample, vast, intense; from this time forward he had to be recognized as the master of a system which would become revealed little by little to the initiated and the extraordinary majesty of which was felt even by the unbelievers.

As Richard Wagner has himself told us in his autobiography, it was in a mood of painful and exuberant excitement, a feverish exaltation, that he composed *Tannhäuser*, the inspiration of which had come to him, majestic and consoling, during the hopeless days and nights of his exile in Paris. Through *Tannhäuser*, he escaped from actual life and its little trivial joys, and soared into an ethereal region, a new and glorious world.

However, as Wagner was soon to discover for himself, this work, begotten in suffering, was destined to beget suffering in its turn. Wagner afterwards declared that in writing it he had written his own death sentence. He had not yet learned that the highest honors are often purchased at the cost of the longest and most frightful martyrdoms.

The friction between Wagner and the Intendant, his official superior, had meanwhile been increasing. The campaign waged by the Dresden newspapers against this pioneer in a sublime art had begun to bear its unwholesome fruit. In spite of the sympathizers he had already gained for his drama, and some of them were most zealous, the kapellmeister could not help recognizing that he had failed in his daring attempt to awaken souls to the sovereign sway of purity and beauty. It was with no little bitterness that he became aware of the unfriendliness of most of the members of the court circle, the timid spirit of some, the indifference of others.

How very few disciples he met along his path, but on the other hand, what hosts of Pharisees! Accordingly there was nothing surprising in Richard Wagner's attitude in regard to the insurrection which broke out in Dresden during the Revolution of 1848. It was evidently far less on account of his social and political views, than for the sake of the new world of sensations and ideas that he was striving to establish by the overthrow of idols in the form of traditional rules for the opera, that Wagner looked upon the Revolution primarily as the dawn of an era fertile in the betterment of individuals and peoples. The fate of his music seemed to him to be closely allied with the desire for independence.

Accordingly, Wagner allied himself with the leaders of the movement, such as Bakunin, who incidentally was never under any misapprehension as to the true character of this exalted idealist's revolutionary views. He collaborated on the *Volksblätter* edited by his friend Rölker, and having drafted a *Plan for a National German Theater,* for the kingdom of Saxony, he delivered a stirring address in behalf of it before a patriotic club, known as the *Vaterlandsverein,* in the course of which he recognized the authority of the king, but eloquently advocated republican ideals.

What was the part played by Wagner in the riot which broke out at Dresden and was rapidly repressed by Prussian bayonets?

There has been as much exaggeration on the one side as on the other. That he would have consented to set fire to the theater, as has been asserted, through his being confused with a pastry-cook also bearing the name of Wagner, one that is exceedingly common in Germany, is manifestly untrue. But it is certain that

Wagner willingly placed himself at the service of the insurgents. Are we to conclude that it was he who sounded the tocsin from the tower with his own hand? It has never been proved. In any case, his sanguinary zeal does not seem to have been very formidable. The sculptor Kietz informed one of the foremost authorities of Wagnerian literature, Mr. Chamberlain, that the author of *Tannhäuser* took him with him to the top of the tower in order to see the view and hear to better advantage the effect of the bells blending with the thunder of the artillery. Another witness, Dr. Thum, relates that he also had a conversation with Wagner on the summit of that same tower, on the subject of—music and philosophy, Beethoven and Berlioz!

Accordingly Wagner was able to affirm, with entire good faith, that his participation in politics was always of an artistic nature.

The revolution in Dresden lasted only a few days (April 28th to May 8th, 1849), and the activities of the Prussian troops, sent to put down the provisional government, resulted altogether in not more than thirty victims.

Having compromised himself, Wagner stayed for a time at Chemnitz, in the home of his brother-in-law, Wolfram. But when he learned that an order for his arrest had been issued, he yielded to the advice of his friends and took steps to reach the frontier. Among others, Franz Liszt, who was one of his earliest admirers, gave him hospitality, and provided him with a passport, bearing the name of a certain Dr. Widemann.

It is stated that Wagner's first intention was to cross over to England. But he stopped at Zurich, then proceeded to Paris, where he remained only a short time, during May and June; after which he installed himself at Zurich.

This was the beginning of the fertile period of his exile, which lasted for a dozen years (1849-1861). Wagner had now found himself and had attained the full maturity of his creative powers. He was destined, during these years of exile, to achieve, in dreamy and melancholy peace, or in the exhausting effort of final consecration, imperishable masterpieces, bearing the hall-mark of his vast and imperious genius.

Sir,

In September last I sent you by Sir George Smart an ouverture entitled Rule Britannia, in order that it might be performed in the concerts of the philharmonic society. Six months have passed since that time without my having recieved any intelligence from you. I beg you will be so good as to inform me, what has been done in regard to my composition.

I remain

Your most obedient servant
Richard Wagner.

Paris, the 12 april 1840.

/. 25. rue de Helder
à Paris /

FACSIMILE LETTER BY WAGNER

## CHAPTER III

**THE GENESIS OF A WORK OF ART—AN ASYLUM: AN OASIS IN THE DESERT—A ROMANTIC LOVE—FROM REAL LIFE TO THE WORLD OF THOUGHT AND OF ART**

IN leaving Dresden, Wagner abandoned a settled, and on the whole a brilliant position. Nevertheless, yielding to what he afterwards called the omnipotence of folly, he had conceived the idea that Dresden was likely to become "the tomb of his art." Accordingly, he resigned himself to exile and retirement, preoccupied with the single purpose of accomplishing his task, and quite indifferent to riches and honors. Study, the joy of meditating and philosophizing, the confidence of a few chosen friends, who faithfully awaited the fruition of his original thoughts, a sufficiently warm dressing gown, a good piano and the attachment of his pet dog and parrot, were to him amply sufficient.

But Minna Wagner, from this time forth, took an entirely different view of their mode of existence. So long as he had occupied an enviable position, she had not been unreasonably disturbed by her husband's chimerical dreams and by an idealism so ill adapted to the immediate needs of his contemporaries. But now she regarded it as sheer folly for him to turn deliberately aside from the beaten path, and devote himself, as he was now doing, to the preaching of a new gospel. All that her husband said or wrote, his music, his slightest actions seemed to her the conduct of a visionary. Furthermore, she suffered from the loss of those material advantages, with which Wagner, absorbed in his dreams, could so easily dispense. "I shall never turn my art-works into merchandise," he once wrote to Liszt, who from the first had estimated him at his true value. But Minna Wagner was far from sharing a philosophy so utopian in its conceptions.

She rejoined her husband at Zurich from a sense of conjugal duty, but with a secret hope that he would awaken to a clearer perception of reality and strive for pecuniary success.

On the contrary, Wagner became more and more engrossed in his proud, uncompromising cult of beauty. With a sort of dogged obstinacy, he grew more and more averse to making concessions. It was no longer a *Rienzi* that occupied him; he dreamed of a vast, crowded, mighty work, impossible perhaps ever to stage, but at least conforming to his ideals. He considered the possibilities of such subjects as *Achilles, Frederick Barbarossa, The Death of Siegfried;* he dreamed of a *Jesus of Nazareth*, which was later metamorphosed into *Parsifal.*

But before finally consecrating himself to the composition of his great musical dramas, Wagner must needs develop his own artistic creed, and proclaim the principles of his æsthetics in a series of special articles, in which he could explain himself at leisure. First came *Art and Revolution,* and *The Art-Work of the*

*Future* (1849), after which he published *Art and Climate, Judaism in Music,* in which he attacked Meyerbeer (1850), *Opera and Drama,* the most important of his writings along this line of thought, and *A Communication to My Friends*.

Meanwhile Liszt, who was Wagner's herald, and whose friendship, Wagner insisted, was the greatest event of his life, taught the public at Weimar to appreciate and applaud the earlier works of this genius who was destined to achieve a greater and finer development amidst the solitude of the picturesque Swiss valleys, or in the society of fellow thinkers.

Zurich, as it happened, being a university town, was at this time the center of a choice intellectual group. Among others, Wagner here once more encountered Semper, the court architect at Dresden, who was also in exile, and who later on was destined to build the Bayreuth Theater. There were, besides, poets such as Herweg, and philologists such as Ettmuller; also, he there made the acquaintance of Challemel-Lacour, who later translated some of his works and became one of the most judicious Wagnerians in France.

Although Wagner held himself aloof mistrustfully, he nevertheless met a number of people who were eager to prove their admiration by doing him services. In this respect special mention should be made of the First Secretary of State, Sulzer, who gave Wagner generous financial aid, and Frau Julia Ritter, who for five years secured him a small annual income, and whose sons, all talented musicians, were brilliant partisans of this still unappreciated master. And we must not forget to mention, among the most zealous apostles of Wagnerism, Klindworth, Draesaeke, Theodore Uhlig, and the most ardent of them all, Wagner's one true pupil, Hans von Bülow.

Since these years of exile at Zurich are essential for an understanding of the life of Wagner and the development of his works, we could not do better than to conjure up the physiognomy of the great musician, as recorded at this epoch by trustworthy witnesses. Frau Eliza Wille, a woman of keen intelligence and a talented writer, has published a number of the master's letters, together with her own recollections and explanatory notes. They form documents of the first importance.

In 1851, Dr. François Wille, a philosopher and journalist, came with his family to Switzerland, as the result of reverses brought about by the Revolution of 1848, and established himself at Mariafeld, distant about a league from Zurich. Frau Wille had previously known Wagner in Dresden, in 1843, at the time of the production of the *Flying Dutchman,* and his image remained graven on her memory: "That graceful and slender figure, that head with its massive brow, the piercing eye and the strong lines of energy deeply imprinted around the small, decided mouth." A painter one evening called her attention to the straight and prominent chin that looked as though carved from marble and gave the musician's face its characteristic expression.

Wagner called upon the Willes at Mariafeld for the first time, in May, 1852, but it was a visit which he was to repeat frequently, sometimes with the poet Herweg, sometimes with his wife, whom Frau Wille has described as a most solicitous housekeeper, but at this time still much agitated by the stormy scenes of the insurrection, a woman who loved the society of her compatriots, but vastly below the level of her husband.

The Willes' home was the meeting-place for discussions of art, literature and philosophy. Carlyle and Schopenhauer were both favorite topics, especially the latter, whose profound and satiric writings had made an enormous impression upon Wagner. On one occasion he burst out laughing, after having read some one of the philosopher's Mephistophelian comments upon women, and observed, "He certainly must have known my wife, Minna!" Wagner became one of Schopenhauer's adherents, notwithstanding that Schopenhauer encouraged him to cultivate letters at the expense of music.

The doctrines of renouncement, sacrifice and abnegation are quite as much a part of the philosopher of Frankfort and his reconstructed Buddhism, as they are of Christianity.

At Mariafeld, Wagner played fragments of *Tannhäuser* and *Lohengrin* and expounded the character of the *Ninth Symphony*. Let us once again listen to Frau Eliza Wille, whose recollections are extremely instructive:

"These gentlemen (Wille and one of his friends) once more plunged into natural history and philological discussions. Hereupon Wagner came over and joined us. 'Good,' said he, 'those two have started in again, digging up roots; they will be at it for a long time.' He began to laugh, then seated himself at the piano. I can never forget the way in which, before beginning, he explained the *Ninth Symphony* to us and made us realize the necessity of the Chorus and the Hymn to Joy as a crowning touch to this magnificent tone-poem. Under his fingers the key-board became a veritable orchestra. Suddenly he paused and said to me,

'Now, listen: the Muses are entering. Amid warlike accents they are leading a phalanx of young men.' Since then I have frequently heard the *Ninth Symphony* rendered by a full orchestra, but that *Allegro vivace alla marcia* I have never heard but *once*. No conductor, no orchestra has been able to make me hear the firm, light step of the Muses as Wagner did, *pianissimo*, moving over the clouds and approaching with a sure and sustained movement. Ah! how that magnificent revelation of the rhythm emanated from that marvelous world of sounds! . . . A single pulsation more or less, and the soul of the listener soars aloft or remains inert!

"Wagner's manner was grave, self-contained, and yet very gracious. One of our friends, an elderly lady, very placid and not easily aroused out of her tranquillity, was fairly electrified when, in a burst of enthusiasm, he intoned with sovereign power:

'Seid umschlungen, Millionen.'

"But all at once he interrupted himself: 'I cannot play the piano, you know,' he said. 'You do not applaud. Now finish it yourselves.'"

It was also at Mariafeld that Wagner first read his *Nibelung's Ring*, before giving a reading of it at the Hotel Bauer, in Zurich.

In 1853 Liszt made his appearance in Wagner's house. Wille asked him if he could not use his influence at the Court at Weimar, in order to make it possible for Wagner to return to Germany. Liszt replied that he knew of no position and of no theater that would be suited to Wagner's needs. Scenery, orchestra, singers would all have to be created expressly for him. Wille observed that such an enterprise would cost not less than a million. Thereupon Liszt cried out in French, as was his habit when overexcited, "He shall have it! The million shall be found!" That was an occasion when Liszt showed himself to be a good prophet.

Frau Wille, to whom we owe these details, took supper on evenings at the Wagners', together with other friends. At dessert, the master of the house disappeared, and returned presently wearing the uniform of the King of Saxony's *Kapellmeister,* his form bent and a sarcastic smile upon his lips. He turned to the guests with a facetious air, and addressing his wife, said, "Yes, yes, Minna, it was all very fine and you liked me this way. It is too bad, poor girl, that the uniform has grown too small for me!" And, in point of fact, that uniform was too small for him!

Misanthropic though he was, Wagner had to recognize that there were a great many people in Zurich who not only esteemed him but had an enthusiastic admiration for him. The concerts which he gave at the Zurich theater brought him veritable ovations. One old musician, a violinist, declared, in speaking of Wagner, "When he is present, it makes another man of me, a different order of musician."

But although Wagner, with his hypersensitive organism, suffered more than another would from home-sickness for the fatherland,

and from the fact that he had not received in Germany the recognition which his artistic pride demanded, it would not be just to say that his years in Zurich taught him the poignant agonies of exile. Every man to whom he spoke, records Frau Wille, felt himself honored; and all the musicians looked up to him as to a master who had opened up new and wonderful paths to music. In spite of his occasional spells of anger and melancholy, he seems to have been treated with a regard verging upon veneration.

In the number of friends who exerted themselves actively in his behalf, special stress should be laid upon his acquaintance with Herr Wesendonck and his wife. Herr Wesendonck was a wealthy merchant who represented a large firm of silk manufacturers in New York. He had settled at Zurich in 1851. Being fond of the arts, he took a keen interest in the destiny of the exiled musician. Frau Wesendonck was only twenty-five years old at the time of her first meeting with Wagner in 1852,

THE WORLD OF ART 69

and possessed a delicate and sensitive nature and a rare artistic temperament.

A pleasant intimacy, a sort of tender and idealistic attachment, soon sprang up between the great and still misunderstood composer, striving in obscurity to bring about the proud accomplishment of his gigantic task, and this docile pupil and devoted friend.

Towards evening, he used to go to play for her on the piano, often pieces of his own composition, based upon poems which she had entrusted to his lofty and melancholy inspiration. And then he talked to her of his reading and his work.

By this time Wagner had developed the full and complete scheme of the Wagnerian drama, the enchanted frame-work within which he was to embody his pure and heroic visions in transcendent harmonies.

In 1853 he finished the whole of the poem of the *Tetralogy*. That same year, in May, he conducted some concerts in the old theater at Zurich, in which he taught his audiences to know and appreciate certain of his own compositions, in all their shadings and their integrity. As a matter of fact, there had been times when Wagner was forced, through want of money, to consent to have his works produced in various foreign cities, where for various reasons great harm was done him through changes and cuts in both text and music, because they insisted upon regarding his works as operas of a singular sort, and not as dramas developed in accordance with a new formula and system.

In 1854 Wagner completed the Prologue to *The Nibelung's Ring*. This same year *Tannhäuser* was produced at Zurich. The year following he visited London, for the purpose of conducting the concerts of the Philharmonic Society there, and while in London he met Berlioz.

After his return to Zurich, Wagner devoted himself to the composition of *Siegfried* and the *Walkyrie*. These prodigious masterpieces he accomplished, in spite of the unhappiness of his domestic life. His wife not only was a sick woman, but she was incapable of understanding the gigantic and tumultuous power of his creations in art, poetry and metaphysics, and furthermore she cherished a vindictive jealousy. As a matter of fact, Wagner had abandoned himself more and more to his intimacy, —a wholly ideal, radiant and consoling intimacy,—with Frau Wesendonck, who sustained his energy, shared his moments of exaltation and lavished upon him the treasures of her unwavering faith. Both she and her husband surrounded the great man with attentions and ungrudgingly gave him their enthusiastic and devoted support.

The house in which Wagner was living was close to that of a tinker, who made a fearful noise, hammering on his anvil. It was unpleasant music at the best, but especially so to the sensitive ears of Wagner. It is related that he finally made up his mind to try to come to terms with the worthy artisan; but the latter replied, "Each one to his own trade, Herr Kapellmeister; I beat my anvil and you beat time. I have no wish to stop you."

Wesendonck kindly suggested that Wagner should have the benefit of a small house belonging to him and quite close to the splendid villa which his own family was to occupy, in the suburbs of Zurich, on what was known as the Green Hill. Wagner joyously accepted and promptly transferred himself thither, together with his wife, his parrot Jacquot and his dog Peps. Here he had a study in which he enjoyed the most delightful security, comfort and quiet, and from the windows of which his gaze could wander over the lake and the wonderful panorama of the Alps. It was in this retreat, where he had foreseen that he would find the necessary tranquillity, that he began the composition of *Tristan and Isolde;* the first act was finished by the end of the year 1857.

But before long he realized that the passion which he cherished for Mathilde Wesendonck was growing stronger; while she, on her side, found it hard to resist the emotions inspired in her by the noble soul and bursting heart of the great musician. Wagner found himself in the romantic position of a second Werther, but with this difference, that he himself was married and that his wife, growing more and more jealous, constantly quarreled with him, and even went so far as to demand explanations from Frau Wesendonck.

How was this romantic love of the great idealist destined to end? Neither he nor his enthusiastic pupil abandoned themselves to a culpable passion. Their relations ended quite philosophically, without suicide or intrigue, but with a total and definitive renouncement. Lichtenberger has analyzed with much delicacy this episode in the life of the great poet-musician: "This drama," he says, "which was wholly internal and unspoken, and which no one except a very small number of his most intimate friends even suspected, at the time when it was taking place, awakened in Wagner's heart some of the most intense and sublime emotions of which the human soul is capable."

And Frau Wesendonck contented herself with writing: "Wagner voluntarily left the asylum which he loved. In witness of that period we have his great work, *Tristan and Isolde*. The rest is mystery and respectful silence."

While Mathilde Wesendonck sought for peace in the calm round of household duties, Minna Wagner waged bitter battles with angry creditors and finally returned home to her own family in Saxony.

Richard Wagner was destined to find his consolation in his art. His secret anguish was already exalted in *Tristan;* and the mystic love which blossomed in his later works and more especially in *Parsifal* was an immortal echo of the deep hidden and painful emotions of the troubled days of his exile in Zurich.

It is possible also that Wagner had other motives for wishing to leave Switzerland. Both as man and artist, as he has himself phrased it, he was journeying towards a new world. Having entered upon a period of conscious artistic purpose,—to employ in our turn the Wagnerian terminology,—and finding a return to favor denied him by the king of Saxony, he now felt a profound desire to leave his silent retreat and reveal his genius to the light of day. Accordingly, it is easy to understand how some of his biographers, and even some of the most conscientious, have chosen to pass over in silence this episode of his romantic love. Wagner not only had "volcanoes in his brain," as Liszt has said, but, according to the wise observation of M. Ad. Jullien, he also had them in his heart. And it was not until a later date that he was destined to achieve domestic happiness. Nor was the joy of triumphing in his art to be granted him until after a new series of formidable trials.

## CHAPTER IV

RICHARD WAGNER GREETED WITH HISSES—THE SPLENDOR AND MISERY OF AN ARTIST—BETWEEN CHARYBDIS AND SCYLLA—ON THE WAY TO SUCCESS—A KING OF DREAMS AND MYSTERIES

IT was in a vein of bitter humor, and while suffering from hunger and the agony of suspense, that Richard Wagner wrote, at the time of his first stay in Paris: "O Poverty, cruel misery, accustomed companion of German artists, it is thou whom I shall invoke first of all in writing these fervent memories! I wish to glorify thee, my faithful patroness, who hast accompanied me always and everywhere; thou, whose brazen arm has saved me from the assaults of prosperity which is full of deception, thou who hast so carefully sheltered me from its ardent rays behind thy dark and heavy cloud, constantly hiding from my eyes the mad vanities of the world. Yes, I am very grateful for thy material interest, but couldst thou not for the future bestow it upon some other protégé? Out of sheer curiosity, I should be glad, if only for a single day, to enjoy the pleasures of existence without any aid from thee. Forgive me, austere goddess, for cherishing this small ambition, but thou knowest the bottom of my heart, thou knowest with what sincere devotion I shall always worship at thy shrine, even if I cease to be thy favorite, the object of thy preference. Amen."

This humorous prayer, which was really a cry of hidden pain, was only half heeded by the inconstant goddess, for during his second sojourn in Paris and also throughout his long and weary wanderings (1859-1864) he experienced many a day of hard privation, which disappointment and the pain of being misunderstood, calumniated, and hated made him feel all the more keenly, nothwithstanding his pride in his genius and his intrepid courage. It must be confessed that his extravagant tastes and his prodigality were a big disadvantage to him, and in some cases did him no small harm.

The whole life of this most powerful dramatist of modern times was itself made up of a series of dramas, each composed of innumerable acts. In following Richard Wagner to Paris for a second time, and then to Vienna and Munich, we are really witnessing a tragedy in three parts, three separate stage-settings.

It was in the autumn of 1859 that Wagner returned to Paris, which it was still his dream to conquer. This time he came with his hands full of works which, if not already famous, had at least received the endorsement of serious artistic successes. He had the admiration of the chosen few, and all the elements essential to success.

He installed himself at the start in the Champs-Elysées, on the Avenue Matignon. For does not fortune smile most graciously upon those who are fortunate to start with? And this time Wagner had not come to Paris to search his path and vegetate on the proceeds of obscure hack-work, but to produce a work that represents one of the mightiest efforts of his vast genius, namely *Tannhäuser*.

A short time later he hired a private dwelling, previously occupied by the author of *The Romance of a Poor Young Man*, Octave Feuillet. It was situated on the Rue Newton, No. 16, near the Avenue du Bois de Boulogne and what was then known as the Barrière de l'Etoile. The building has since been demolished. Wagner furnished it mainly with objects that he brought from his retreat in Zurich, and that conjured up tender memories of the charming Mathilde Wesendonck.

In his personal recollections, M. E. Michotte has recorded a good many precise details as to the more striking characteristics of the great composer's habits and mode of life at this time. He lived in a tranquil and modest fashion. Aside from a short walk in the Bois de Boulogne, whither he went accompanied by a bright and lively little dog, whose antics amused him, he passed his time in working, either with Edmond Roche on the French translation of *Tannhäuser*, or giving the finishing touches to his *Tetralogy*.

Minna Wagner had once again returned to her conjugal duties, and is described at this time as a person of middle-class appearance, simple and self-effaced.

Wagner, bold innovator that he was, had come to Paris hoping to find the atmosphere necessary to the success of his art, and he had the good fortune, almost immediately after his arrival, to form some valuable and comforting friendships. Roche, who was a poet and musician of some talent, was working one day rather sadly in the office of the Customs Department, when he overheard a heated discussion. A foreigner, a German, was protesting vigorously against some of the formalities to which that department is still only too ready, alas, to force us to submit! The stranger gave his name, Richard Wagner. Roche at once hastened to intervene and smooth away the difficulties.

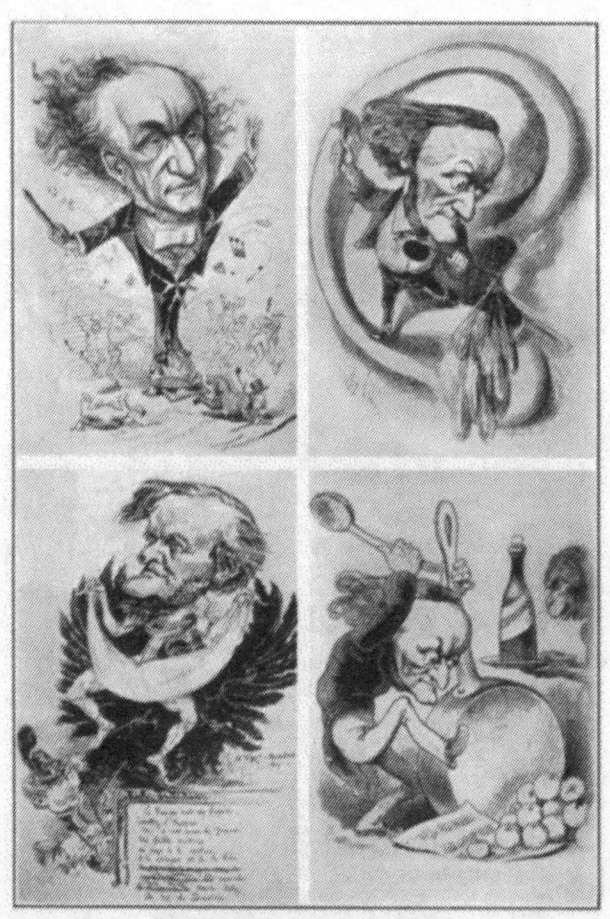

### WAGNER IN CARICATURE
*Above*: Caricature by Faustin (London *Figaro*, 1876), and by Gill (*Eclipse*, 1876). *Below:* Wagner as Première Danseuse, by Tiret-Bognet (1891); Wagner the Tetralogist, by Gill (1876)

When Wagner sought to express his gratitude, Roche declared that he had been only too happy to have been of service to so great an artist.

"What, you know me then?" asked Wagner, surprised and delighted. Roche smiled and began to hum softly some airs from *Tannhäuser* and *Lohengrin*.

"Ah," cried Wagner, "what a happy omen! The first Parisian whose acquaintance I make knows my music. I must write and tell Liszt at once. Monsieur, we shall meet again." And he forthwith sent Roche a present of several pieces of music which he unearthed from his trunks and on which he inscribed a dedication.

We shall meet Roche again among the few friends who used to gather around Wagner at his house on Wednesday evenings, and who included Gasperini, Champfleury, one of his warmest partisans, Gustave Doré, Emile Ollivier and his wife, the daughter of Liszt, Stephen Heller, Villot, superintendent of the imperial museums, Berlioz, Jules Ferry, de

Lorbac, Charles Baudelaire, the great poet of *Fleurs du Mal,* who was one of the first to write a splendid analysis of the romantic art of Richard Wagner.

Hans von Bülow soon added himself to the number of the initiated, and used to play for them on the piano, rendering with extraordinary mastery portions of *Tannhäuser* and *Tristan.*

Wagner was able to express himself quite fluently in French, and he used to amaze his guests with his furious eloquence, the loftiness of his views on topics of the most diverse sort, as well as by his witticisms, and unexpected and often highly picturesque anecdotes.

He interpreted his own works with surprising vigor, and his declamation was uncommonly powerful. His voice, on the other hand, was not always true. The master had no illusions in this respect and freely admitted that a composer with so inharmonious a voice was enough to put to flight all the master singers of the world, including those of Nuremberg.

It is well known that Wagner made no claim of being a better pianist than he was a singer, and no doubt for good reason.

Gasperini has related that the author of *Tannhäuser* once invited the director of the Théâtre Lirique to come and hear the score of his opera:

"Wagner battled with the formidable *finale* of the second act; he sang, he cried, he raved, he played with his hands, his wrists, his elbows, he smashed the pedals and bruised the keys. In the midst of this chaos, M. Carvalho remained as impassive as the man of whom Horace told, waiting with a patience worthy of antiquity for the pandemonium to cease. When Wagner had finished, M. Carvalho murmured a few words of thanks, turned on his heel and disappeared."

Wagner determined to get the profane public into training before producing *Tannhäuser*. The Théâtre des Italiens was hired for the sum of eight thousand francs, exclusive of the cost of the orchestra and the lighting, and the first of three Wagner concerts was given there on January 25th, 1860.

The first half of the program consisted of the overture to the *Flying Dutchman* and selections from *Tannhäuser*, and the second half included the prelude to *Tristan and Isolde* and selections from *Lohengrin*.

Without dwelling too much upon the reception accorded at that time to Wagner's music, and upon the division of audience, critics and composers into two camps, we will cite the following ironic portrait of Wagner, drawn by the incisive pen of Fiorentino, and published in the *Constitutionnel*:

"He has a fine, noble and lofty brow, but the lower part of his face is weak and vulgar. One would say that two fairies, the one malicious and the other kind and affectionate, had presided at his birth. The fairy of harmony caressed and beautified the brow from which so many daring conceptions and mighty thoughts were destined to come forth; the fairy of melody, foreseeing the harm which this child would do her, seated herself upon his face and flattened his nose."

The audience was made up of artists, musicians and persons of social prominence; and there were many Germans present. Wagner was warmly applauded, and even those of his hearers who were least inclined to be enthusiastic found themselves forced to accord him their frank admiration after seeing him stand for three hours, baton in hand, conducting both the orchestra and the choruses from memory, without music-rack or score.

This concert, which earned Wagner a number of fervent friendships and a few implacable enmities, was followed by two others, on the 1st and 8th of February respectively. M. J. G. Prud'homme records that the deficit for these three performances amounted to the sum of ten thousand francs, which was paid by Mme. de Moukhanoff.

Another event, more important, not to say

86   RICHARD WAGNER

momentous, was the famous production of *Tannhäuser* at the Opéra, March 13, 1861.

It was all in vain that Wagner made calls upon the most celebrated composers of the period, since irritable and nervous as he was, he had allowed himself to express a multitude of caustic judgments regarding them. He must needs seek to secure some other influences. The most efficacious seems to have been that of the Princesse de Metternich, for it was thanks to her, so the statement goes, that the Maréchal Maignan undertook to interest the Emperor on Wagner's behalf.

Roche had now been working for a whole year on his French translation of *Tannhäuser*. Sunday, his one day of freedom from the custom-house, he was in the habit of spending with Wagner. On the basis of Roche's own account, Victorien Sardou has pictured that terrible man, striding up and down, with blazing eye and furious gesture, pounding on the piano as he passed it, singing, shouting, and repeating to his harassed collaborator:

"Go on, go on!"

And when finally the latter was forced to sue for mercy, he asked in surprise:

"What is the matter?"

"I am hungry," answered the unhappy poet.

After swallowing a mouthful of food, the two would return to their task; and as twilight set in, poor Roche could see, as in a sort of nightmare, a huge, stooping shadow that seemed to dance around him, in the flickering light of the lamp, still pounding on his infernal piano, constantly shouting, "Go on, go on!" and wearying his ears with cabalistic phrases and notes imported from the lower regions.

The first rehearsal took place September 24th, 1860. But it was not until after a hundred and sixty-four rehearsals, a number which provoked the merriment of journalists and caricaturists, that the first public performance was given.

Everything had been done on a truly magnificent scale. The leading singers, the tenor Niemann, the baritone Morelli, Mmes. Tedesco and Marie Sasse were of the foremost rank; the stage settings were sumptuous.

But Wagner had aroused all sorts of hostility, against his work, against his reforms in music and the theater, even against himself personally. A clique had been formed, composed chiefly of members of the Jockey Club, and the uproar they made rendered a hearing of the opera impossible. Wagner's tempestuous nature, his aggressive publications, the more or less disguised hostility of the French composers, his own unwisdom in writing the bacchanale of the Venusberg in the symphonic style of his latest works, and offering it to his audience by way of a ballet after the overture, were quite enough, aside from certain reasons of a political nature, to explain Wagner's failure and what amounted to a riot. It should be added that, in spite of the fervor of the initiated few, a band of independent and audacious artists, the French public was not yet ready to understand such complicated instrumentation, nor the distinctly Germanic nature

## SPLENDOR AND MISERY 89

of the theme celebrated by this new genius.

For the second performance Wagner made certain modifications in the passages which had provoked hilarity. There was less laughter but more disturbance, thanks to an assortment of hunting whistles purchased from an armorer in the Passage de l'Opéra and distributed among the members of the Jockey Club. The presence of the emperor and empress in no wise deterred this demonstration, against which a good many people arose in protest, and which called forth an eloquent and indignant denunciation from Charles Baudelaire. Similar scenes of violence greeted the third performance, and Berlioz asserts with evident satisfaction that Wagner was publicly hailed as a knave, a blackguard and an idiot.

Although the receipts amounted to 10,790 francs, 60 centimes, Wagner, acting upon the advice of his friends, withdrew *Tannhäuser*. In addition to Baudelaire, other writers such as Théophile Gautier, Vacquerie and Catulle Mendès. undertook to defend the insulted artist, who for the next six months signed his letters, "The hissed author of *Tannhäuser*." And Jules Janin, the critic on the *Débats,* suggested a picturesque coat-of-arms for those members of the Jockey Club who had made the demonstration: "a whistle, on a field of howling throats."

Notwithstanding that he answered the attacks of his adversaries in a fierce and incisive manner, and that he suffered from this outcome which cruelly aggravated his financial difficulties, Wagner could at least console himself with the fact that he had been estimated at his real value, as poet, musician and dramatist, by a select minority of the French public. And that, too, at a time when in Germany he was for the most part more discussed than honored, and where they hesitated to produce such costly spectacles. Nevertheless the author of *Tannhäuser* was profoundly hurt in his pride as an artist, and more especially a German artist, and he made the mistake of nursing the memory of his enemies rather than his sympathizers, in connection with these experiences in France.

Austria, whither he next went, was far less hospitable to him. Vienna appeared to him as the capital city of true frivolity, and although *Lohengrin* had been applauded there, he had to renounce the pleasure of seeing *Tristan* produced. Paris, on the other hand, in spite of the bitterness of a defeat which was perhaps more apparent than real, had left him, to borrow his own phrase, "some encouraging memories."

Vienna, on the contrary, was a solitude in which he felt misunderstood and discouraged. Evidently condemned to a wandering life, Wagner now returned to Paris and remained there incognito for two months (December and January, 1861-1862), living on the Quai Voltaire, and working on the text of the *Meistersinger*. He passed the ensuing year at Biberich, on the banks of the Rhine. Then he returned to Austria, making it the starting point for a trip to Russia, where he gave several concerts at Moscow and St. Petersburg (1863), and for visits to Budapest and Prague, to superintend the production of his works.

M. Adolphe Jullien, whose writings on Wagner are authoritative, relates that he was very well received at court and that his concerts brought him in a considerable sum. But like many another artist, Wagner took little pains to economize. With the true instinct of the theatrical profession, he loved all things that pleased the eye, and especially fabrics that lent themselves to harmonious folds.

A Viennese dressmaker of high repute, Fräulein Bertha, made him dressing-gowns and jackets of pink, pale blue and flaming red satin, with lilac or orange ribbons. Lace shirts and satin shoes completed the princely flamboyance of his attire. According to letters dating from 1864 to 1867, the cost of these furnishings amounted in a single year to eight thousand francs. This correspondence betrays the fact that his love of luxury was far greater than his desire to pay his bills promptly.

Without indulging in useless comments, we need not be greatly surprised to find that his financial condition was greatly aggravated. Meanwhile the campaign against this reformer of the operatic stage continued to bear bitter fruit. He was accused of the most heinous misdeeds. At this time he was living in a small house at Penzing on the outskirts of Vienna. Nevertheless, he was reproached for luxurious living and abominable misconduct, even for the champagne which he drank to calm the state of his disordered nerves. Yet in reality, notwithstanding his expensive tastes, he sought his true pleasures in the full development of his musical dramas. His experience as a dramatist had served only to increase his zeal for revolutionizing both the musical technique of the opera and its methods of portraying human emotions. If he failed to achieve works in full accordance with his desires during these years of trial, he nevertheless abandoned none of his gigantic conceptions, nor marred them by a single concession. But how is an artist to struggle against the self-interest of some and the settled habits of others, and establish a new system in the art of evoking the beautiful, when he is destitute of resources and must slave desperately merely for the purposes of keeping himself alive? For, after a few profitable engagements and brilliant performances, Wagner had once more dropped back into silence and isolation.

Hounded by his creditors and wearied by so many useless efforts, he left Austria, returned to Switzerland, and took refuge with the Wille family, at Mariafeld.

Frau Eliza Wille welcomed her illustrious and unhappy guest with charming graciousness. All he wanted was to be let alone and to work in peace upon the last portion of his *Meistersinger*. She pictures him to us striding up and down the terrace in front of the villa, in his long tunic of brown velvet and with his black cap on his head, looking like some patrician who has just stepped out of an engraving by Albrecht Dürer.

## SPLENDOR AND MISERY 95

This exceptional woman saw that the energetic and unconquerable Richard Wagner was now broken down, weary of work, unable to control himself. In addition to the tortures which his own imagination inflicted on him, and the wretched state of his finances, the causes of his present prostration were legion. His irritability had estranged him from his family and his life-long friends. As for Frau Minna Wagner, she had gone back to her own family in Dresden.

Wagner was worried by his inability to give his wife financial aid. But one day he showed Frau Wille a letter and said that now he could send the money, since the people in Paris were honest enough to pay a royalty to a composer whose works they had publicly produced. Then, becoming excited, he cried out:

"Everything would have gone well between my wife and me, if I had not spoiled her so deplorably. . . . She could not understand that a man like me cannot live if his wings are fettered. What did she know of the divine rights of passion, which I have proclaimed by the blazing funeral pyre of the Walkyrie, banished from heaven by the gods! Love sacrifices itself in death, that is the significance of the *Götterdämmerung*."

It was in vain that Frau Wille lent him books on Napoleon and Frederick the Great, and the works of the German mystics. It was in vain that she foretold the splendid future which awaited him. But let us listen once again to her own words, for she has admirably described Wagner's attitude and utterances during that painful sojourn at Mariafeld. A biographer is only too lucky to have at his disposal documents of this sort, written in so fine a style and with such rare psychological discernment:

"The sun had just set in all its beauty, and the sky and earth were bathed in light and flame. Wagner said to me:

"'Why do you talk to me of my future, when my manuscripts are still stowed away in the bottom of my closet? Who is going to produce a work of art which I cannot allow to be performed without the collaboration of propitious demons, so that the entire world may know that it is thus that the master conceived it and wished it to be given?'

"In the intensity of his excitement, he was striding back and forth through the room. All of a sudden he paused in front of me and cried out:

" 'I am differently organized, I have more sensitive nerves, I must have beauty, brilliance and light! The world owes me what I need. I cannot live in a miserable position as organist, like your master Sebastian Bach. Am I incredibly exacting in asking for the small amount of luxury which I crave, I who am preparing delight for thousands upon thousands of human beings?'

"As he said this, he raised his head as though he were uttering a challenge, then dropped back into his seat in the window alcove and stared out, straight ahead of him."

In spite of the heart-breaking cares of pecuniary distress that was only too genuine, in spite of sleeplessness and ailments which forced him to adopt a diet and take the waters of Vichy, Wagner returned to his task and to a short respite of hope.

Nevertheless, when he left Mariafeld he said gravely to Frau Wille:

"My friend, you do not know the extent of my misfortunes, nor the depths of wretchedness which await me!"

In taking leave of the village barber, he assured him that he was going away because the latter's prices were too high! The good Figaro of the place replied that he need not leave on that account and that henceforward he would give him bargain rates. Wagner was much amused by this incident, notwithstanding his many anxieties.

Wagner made his way to Stuttgart. At this moment he had reached the acme of discouragement and misfortune. He thought of returning to Russia, and even of setting out for America. But one cannot help believing that his "propitious demons" were watching over Wagner and over his immense and pathetic art. An envoy from the young king, Ludwig II of Bavaria, Herr von Pfistermeister, after having vainly sought him in Vienna and Mariafeld, finally discovered him at Stuttgart, in April, 1864.

This was an immense good fortune for Wagner, and he wrote to tell of it to Frau Eliza Wille, who had helped him to bear so many sorrows and anxieties.

He had just been presented to the king, on the 4th of May:

"The king," he wrote, "is unfortunately so handsome, so intelligent, so ardent and so great that I fear that his life will vanish away from this vulgar world like a fugitive and divine dream. He loves me with the ardor and fervor of first love, he knows and understands all that concerns me. He wants me to remain permanently with him, he wants me to work and to rest and to produce my dramas; he is willing to give me everything that I need; he wants me to finish the *Ring of the Nibelung,* and he is going to have it produced precisely in the way that I desire. I am to be relieved of every pecuniary care; I am to have everything that I want; and the sole condition is that I remain with him."

Thus it was that Wagner became, not the conductor of the Court Theater's orchestra, but the personal friend of this strange sovereign, who craved intellectual intoxication. This dreamer, this mystic, this noble and singular patron of arts and letters saw in Wagnerianism and in the development of the musical drama a source of ecstasies and lofty religious emotions. He understood Wagner as he really was, systematic, obstinate and sublime in his conception of a supreme art; indeed, he understood him better than his best friends did. Even Hans von Bülow and Liszt were less devoted followers than he.

It looked as though Wagner had now come to the end of his humiliations. For was not this king, who had just succeeded to the throne,

## SPLENDOR AND MISERY 101

and was so enamored of Wagner, destined to become his "guardian angel"? And indeed, the path towards triumph did seem to have been made easy; yet Wagner had not yet finished climbing his Calvary. Notwithstanding that Ludwig of Bavaria showed such remarkable faith in him, he still had to contend against the force of tradition and the settled habits of a public which even yet numbered far too many Philistines.

Wagner became all powerful at court. The extraordinary monarch, Ludwig II, began to hoard up his revenues and postponed certain public works undertaken by his father, in order to preserve intact the sum needed for the production of the *Ring of the Nibelung*. Consequently, the great poet-musician was looked upon as the king's favorite. The socialist Lassalle, as well as the parents of a murderess, appealed to him to intercede on their behalf with Ludwig II.

The king appointed Hans von Bülow as his own personal pianist; and Wagner, in a frenzy of joy, looked upon the kindly monarch as a divine being, endowed with the most marvelous faculties.

After having had a representation of *Tannhäuser* at the Court Theater in Munich, he gave a production of the *Flying Dutchman* at the same theater, on the 4th of December, 1864. For a time, Wagner lived in a sort of enchanted dream, which was nevertheless troubled by the clamors of a certain element which criticized the conduct and infatuation of the king. The latter, with unparalleled sureness of purpose, dreamed of nothing but the realization of the Wagnerian drama; and it was under admirable conditions that *Tristan,* an incomparable specimen of Wagnerian art, was produced (May-June, 1865). These performances, to borrow the author's own phraseology, were veritable artistic festivals, conducted with absolutely no regard to the financial outcome of the venture. It was no longer a question of pleasing or not pleasing, but of at last presenting a "solution of pure problems of art." Among the members of the cast, special mention should be made of Schnorr von Carolsfeldt and his wife.

Hans von Bülow had now become conductor at the Court Theater. Wagner and the king, however, were preoccupied with plans for an ideal theater, for the exclusive production of Wagnerian drama, and a small model of which was exhibited to a special public composed of those who showed more or less zeal for the cause.

Meanwhile, the hostility against the monarch and his protégé was increasing and began to be disquieting. While the one was reproached for his prodigality, the other was censured for his unrestrained sybaritism. Journalists circulated calumnies about him, and asserted that "a great oriental potentate could be very well contented with the standard of living set by Wagner."

There is no doubt that Wagner took advantage of his prestige in a lordly way and without scruples. The story is told that the principal upholsterer of the city, to whom he owed a sum equivalent to twenty thousand dollars, waylaid him one day publicly in the theater, and swore that he would not let him go until he had paid his debts. The man raised such an outcry that Wagner was forced to draw him a draft on the royal treasury.

If we are to avoid the charge of partiality, we must admit that such occurrences, even if allowance is made for exaggeration, are characteristic, and explain the anger of the subjects of Ludwig II.

Between him and Wagner a real intimacy existed, and in their intercourse they employed the familiar "thou" and "thee." Ludwig II has left evidence of his affection and his Wagnerian fervor in a letter addressed to a cousin, the fiancée of his dreams, who had once offered him some wild flowers. He tells how he had found on a piano, belonging to relatives of his, the Princesses Max, some of the poet-musician's librettos. He became absorbed in *Lohengrin*. The mystery of the legend appealed to his own mysterious soul:

"How many times," he wrote, "I have seen in imagination the knight and his faithful swan gliding over the waves! There I found my childhood dreams and my youthful fantasies delightfully realized. And these familiar personages spoke to me in rhythms which intoxicated me like the voluptuous perfume of the lindens in bloom."

Let us hear further these strange and noble confessions of the poet-king, who found in the art of Wagner the realization of a pure and religious ideal, who said to him, "You and God," and who assured him of his faithful enthusiasm until even beyond the grave, in the empire of universal death:

"How we became friends, friends in the highest sense of the term, which has been so much abused, the world already knows. And this world, which I have never loved, obliges me to reveal myself continually more and more, because of the manner in which it judges this friendship. What might I not have had to endure from this venial and despicable world, if I had not been King? . . . God in his goodness will leave me the joy which I derive from fostering and carrying out the plans of this dear friend, and from being to him in a small measure what he is to me infinitely."

In order to understand the tone of this mystic admiration, a form of romanticism full of morbid ecstasy, it will suffice to read a letter written by Ludwig II to Wagner after the performance of *Tristan:*

"Great and divine friend, I can hardly wait until tomorrow evening, I am so eager to attend the second performance. . . . My soul longs to be ravished once again by that splendid, lofty, sublime work. All honor to its creator! All glory to him! Will you not assure me, my dear friend, that you will never allow yourself to lose the courage to create new works? In the name of those upon whom you have bestowed a happiness such as God alone can give, I pray of you that you will never cease."

It is not unprofitable to dwell upon the exaltation of this eccentric and unhappy king, for it enables us to define in advance the psychology of Wagnerianism, an almost Europe-wide cult of beauty, which is one of the most striking intellectual events of the end of the nineteenth century.

Under the auspices of Ludwig II of Bavaria, who as a matter of fact made it possible for him to realize his ambitious dreams in all their integrity, Wagner played the rôle of a sort of high priest.

The documents above cited are also of weighty interest from the simple point of view of the musician's biography,—especially if, having shown an adequate appreciation of these impassioned appeals, these intensely poetic avowals, we take the trouble to remember that the sum expended in staging *Tristan and Isolde* at Munich amounted to very nearly forty thousand dollars, and that it had cost over thirty thousand for *Lohengrin*. And it should be added, without fear of exaggeration, that the royal presents, both in money and in specific articles, had cost the Treasury something in the neighborhood of a hundred thousand dollars.

It can easily be imagined that the Bavarian press did not fail to circulate sensational details and to excite the resentment of the public against a king with such a passion for the fine arts. The *Kölnisches Zeitung* announced one day that Ludwig II had just presented his favorite musician with a walking stick, the handle of which was a swan wrought of gold and set with diamonds.

The performance of *Tristan,* which had been hours of enchantment for the king, the author and the initiated few, meant little or nothing to the general public. The author himself stopped them after the fourth.

Eager to escape the "persecution" of the populace of Munich, Wagner withdrew to Geneva. He realized that, in the face of a more or less open animosity, it would be impossible ever to see the theater of his dreams erected in Munich. Accordingly, he decided to live in retirement. But he was not to be forgotten, for Ludwig II remained his faithful friend throughout all the time that he was striving, in obscurity and silence, to complete the creations which were to win the admiration of posterity.

## CHAPTER V

PEACE AND MEDITATION—FROM DREAM TO REALITY—THE APOTHEOSIS OF RICHARD WAGNER

IT was in his retreat at Triebschen, picturesquely situated on the shore of the Lake of the Four Cantons, that Wagner made the first draft of *Parsifal* and finished his *Meistersinger,* the first representation of which took place in June, 1868.

It was a splendid occasion. The king who occupied the central box, had invited the dramatist to sit with him. After the end of the first act there were calls for the author to appear upon the stage, but Wagner was unable to find the way. At the end of the performance, at the request of Ludwig II, he arose from his seat and, from the eminence of the royal box, bowed to the audience.

Nevertheless, from this time forth Wagner

# FROM DREAM TO REALITY 111

avoided the Bavarian capital. The first performances of the *Rhinegold* (September 22, 1869) and the *Walkyrie* (June, 1870), were given without him and suffered from his absence. The king, however, continued to hold him in favor, and it is stated that he paid him a visit incognito at Triebschen.

There Wagner continued to live, in a state of happiness so great that it bordered upon ecstasy. His wife Minna had died, January 25th, 1866, from heart disease, which for a long time had undermined her health, although it is stated that her condition became especially precarious after the failure of *Tannhäuser* at Paris.

The great artist had never found in her that intensity of love, confidence and surrender of which he had dreamed. He once wrote that he would give all his art in return for a woman who would love him without reserve. Such a woman he found in Cosima Liszt, who had married Hans von Bülow, and who left him in order to share the destiny of Wagner. But far from demanding that he should abandon his art, she aided its development. The Bayreuth Festivals were destined to be her work, quite as much as that of Richard Wagner, and she alone had the necessary intelligence and energy to carry on his sacred task and mission.

On this subject let us hear what Wagner himself said, in his last letter to Eliza Wille, dated June 23d, 1870:

"Since I last saw you in Munich (this was at the time of the performance of the *Meistersinger*, two years previous), I have not left my retreat, which since then has been shared by her who was destined to prove that there was something that could be done for me, and that the axiom formulated by so many of my friends, 'There is nothing to be done for Wagner,' was not true. She knew that there was something to do and she has done it. She has braved every ignominy and borne the burden of every condemnation. She has given me a son who is marvelously beautiful and strong, and whom I have boldly named Siegfried. He

THE THEATRE AT BAYREUTH

Interior of the Theatre where the Pilgrims of Art commune in the Wagnerian Religion

is now as flourishing as my works are, and has given me a renewal of life, for at last I have found a reason for living."

Frau Wille herself is the source of some graphic details of Wagner's intimate life during this period of his complex and tumultuous life, —a period as fruitful as that of Zurich, for all that it was more secluded. Neither Frau Wille nor Nietzsche, who spoke so highly of Wagner before he began to disparage him, could conceal their admiration for Frau Cosima, who was a heroic woman and came of a noble race.

"The gifted daughter of Liszt," said Frau Wille, "resembled her illustrious father, and yet with a marked difference. The intelligence, the imagination and the poetry that animated her made her the true companion for Wagner and enabled her to follow him, with full understanding, to all the heights towards which his genius drew him. She absorbed herself in his music with the most devout enthusiasm, for the world in which he lived was also her own.

Wagner often exerted his genius to pay her some delicate and touching tribute in the form of music. In her home life she was wholly devoted to her duties as wife and mother, governess and teacher of her children, as Wagner himself has told me in his letters. Her intellectual culture, her feminine tact, and her knowledge of the world and of life rendered her conversation most attractive."

It can be readily conceived that this atmosphere of alternate serenity and radiant exaltation was essential to Wagner while he was composing his wonderful idyll of *Siegfried* and the greater part of *Götterdämmerung,* not to mention numerous articles, such as *The Art of Conducting, The Aim of Opera,* and *Beethoven.*

We have other picturesque details of the Wagner of the Triebschen period. Catulle Mendès, who had known him when he was living in Paris, in the Rue d'Aumale, suffering from all sorts of privations and anxieties, went to pay him a visit on the shores of Lake Lucerne.

"We had hardly stepped from our conveyance," wrote Mendès, who was accompanied by that rarely gifted poet, Villiers de l'Isle Adam, "when we saw a huge straw hat, and beneath it a pale face, with eyes that glanced restlessly from right to left, as if seeking something. It was he. Somewhat overawed, we stood there looking at him, not venturing to advance. He was small, lean, and closely enveloped in a long frock coat of maroon cloth; and through the suspense of waiting, his whole frail looking body,—which possibly was really very strong, like a bundle of steel springs,— was trembling almost convulsively, like an hysterical woman. But his face retained a magnificent expression of proud serenity. While his mouth, with lips so thin and pale as to be hardly visible, was twisted into the lines of a sour smile, his splendid brow, beneath the hat that was pushed backward, his splendid, vast, pure brow, surmounted by singularly soft hair, already turning gray, that was brushed back, suggested unalterable peace and the pursuit of some immense idea. The moment that he saw us, Richard Wagner quivered from head to foot with the suddenness of a violin string vibrating to the rhythm of a pizzicato, tossed his hat in the air with cries of mad welcome, almost dancing with joy, and flung himself upon us, hung on our necks, seized us by the arm, until hustled, jostled, swept along in a whirlwind of words and gestures, we found ourselves at last in the carriage which was to take us to the master's habitation."

One diverting anecdote is related in connection with this visit of Mendès and Villiers de l'Isle Adam. The two French writers noticed that they were treated by the hotel staff with something more than respectful consideration. The proprietor himself kissed their hands obsequiously. One day, after he had bowed many times, he said to Mendès:

"Sire, Your Majesty's wishes shall be obeyed, and since Your Majesty insists, we shall respect his incognito." They had mistaken him for the king, Ludwig of Bavaria, and Villiers for the Prince of Taxis.

Mendès further shows us Wagner with his black dog and his black cap, or such as tradition has represented him, clad in frock coat, with trousers of golden satin embroidered over with flower designs of pearls. He had a passion for silks and velvet, and luminous fabrics. He moved tremulously; yet he never remained seated, but talked, talked continuously, interspersing his sublime conceptions with puns and witticisms, expounding his dramatic projects and the themes of his plots, and exhausting the vocabulary of terms expressive of pride, tenderness, violence and buffoonery.

His hearers laughed with him, wept with him, taken out of themeslves, seeing his visions, yielding to "the terror and the charm of his speech," as to a cyclone of sun-enveloped dust and tempest.

And undoubtedly Mendès, the belated romanticist, and Villiers, the artist of the scintillating word, were well qualified to understand the hero of romantic art, Richard Wagner.

Mme. Judith Gautier, in her turn, has given us, in the course of her interesting *Souvenirs*, a fine moral portrait of Wagner (July, 1869):

"It must be admitted," she writes, "that there are in Wagner's character a certain violence and rudeness that are responsible for his being so often misunderstood, but only by those who judge solely from outside appearances. Excessively nervous and impressionable as he is, whatever emotion he experiences is carried to the point of paroxysm. A mild disappointment drives him almost to despair; the slightest irritation goads him into fury. His marvelous and exquisitely sensitive organization has passed through terrible crises, and one wonders how he rallies from them; a single day of distress ages him by ten years, but when he is happy again, he is younger than ever within twenty-four hours. He squanders his energies with extraordinary prodigality. He is always sincere, always gives himself up wholly to whatever he is doing; yet at the same time his nature is extremely changeable, and his opinions and ideas, although quite absolute in the beginning, are not in the least irrevocable; no one is readier than he to admit an error, but he must needs wait until the first heat is passed."

Is it not worth while to meditate upon this judicious portrait, in order to have an intelligent understanding of this great artist, who was at one and the same time so greatly adulated and so greatly decried?

Notwithstanding his impulsive temperament, Wagner's life at Triebschen was on the whole very happy and exceedingly fruitful. From eight o'clock in the morning until five in the afternoon he toiled ceaselessly, in the midst of that majestic and fertile Swiss valley. It was during his meditations at Triebschen that the plans were matured for the *Festspielhaus*, that temple of musical drama, of Wagnerian drama, of German drama, which had been Wagner's dream throughout long years. It was to be built at Bayreuth, whither even to this day the Wagnerian pilgrimage wends its way in accordance with the established rites. Wagner himself openly declared that all his prior successes were founded upon misunderstandings and poor performances, and that his reputation was not worth a nut-shell. Accordingly, the dawn of his real glory was destined to date from Bayreuth, where his thoughts were for the first time realized in all their amplitude, in that series of what we may call the Olympic Games of modern Germany.

The laying of the cornerstone of the theater at Bayreuth, built in accordance with the plans drawn by Wagner's old friend, Semper, took place on the 22d of May, 1872, to the accompaniment of a march written by Wagner in 1864, in honor of the king. The town had donated the site. Nietzsche was present and occupied a place of honor beside Frau Cosima Wagner. Ludwig II sent his secretary to give assurance that the royal coffers would always be open for these sublime manifestations,—and in point of fact those coffers were drawn upon, time and again, during the years that followed. The king also sent the following telegram to Wagner:

"My dearest friend, on this day of such important significance to all Germany, I offer you from the very bottom of my heart, my sincerest and most ardent congratulations. Greeting and benediction upon this great enterprise. Today, more than ever, I am one with you in spirit!"

Wagner had good reason for writing, as he did in 1872:

"What the king has done means far more than my life to me. What he has desired and sought on my behalf represents a future of glorious promise. A high intellectual culture, a movement directed towards the noblest destinies of which a nation is capable, that is what the relations between him and me express and represent."

From this time forward, Wagner made his permanent home in a house situated some little distance from the *Festspielhaus*, and which he christened *Wahnfried*, a somewhat enigmatic term and one difficult to translate, but which we may render "freedom from illusions, after so many disappointments," could it not be more appropriately rendered, "the illusion of freedom," since Wagner, as Mr. Chamberlain has remarked, was still destined to suffer from his uncertainty of achieving that absolute, total, definitive success, for which he had prayed, even at Bayreuth, in the glorious years of his old age?

Thanks to the development and activity of the Wagnerian societies, and to the resources furnished by the establishment of a special fund, the cycle of the *Ring of the Nibelung*, conceived by Wagner "in his confidence in the German spirit and completed to the greater glory of his august benefactor, King Ludwig II of Bavaria," was produced in its integrity in 1876. Yet the attachment of his wife and son,

## FROM DREAM TO REALITY 123

and the devotion of the king, of Liszt and several others, such as the Comte de Gobineau and the poet Heinrich von Stein, did not save Wagner from being once again misunderstood.

In spite of the presence of several kings and other highly influential personages, the result had not come up to the expectations of the master. It was, in fact, a material setback. Nevertheless, a second fund was collected and a school of music and lyric declamation was opened. But the success of this was not proportioned to the effort.

In July, 1882, through the aid of a new subscription, and thanks to various liberal donations, the public was admitted to sixteen representations of *Parsifal*, Wagner's crowning work, in which he has developed in heroic form his doctrine of love and regeneration. These performances were followed by six representations of the cycle of the *Ring*.

The number of tickets sold was 8,200, and the gross receipts amounted to 240,000 marks ($60,000).

The money subscribed had not been entirely spent, so a fund was started to meet the expenses of another series of Wagnerian performances, which owed their success quite as much to dilettanteism as to the zeal of Frau Cosima Wagner, and all the partizans and *Wagnervereine* taken together.

Accordingly, in spite of some last anxieties and disappointments, Bayreuth represents the apotheosis of Wagner, the great genius so long decried and reviled, but henceforth glorified in an almost religious manner, in those modern mystery plays of drama and music.

Consequently, it is to Bayreuth that we must turn in order to conjure up the glorious Wagner of these closing years. And first of all the question arises: Why did he choose Bayreuth for the site of a theater which, according to his own statement, was to cost in the neighborhood of $225,000? Wagner's explanation is as follows:

"The choice could not be a capital city nor any town already possessing a theater, nor a bathing resort that during the summer would attract a great crowd of a sort utterly incapable of appreciating such spectacles. It ought to be situated as nearly as possible in the heart of Germany. Besides, I could not choose any other than a Bavarian town, if I was to hope for a place of permanent residence, and it was in Bavaria that I was destined to find it."

Mme. Judith Gautier, a Wagnerian from the earliest hour, one might almost say from her birth, and one who in her writings has paid the highest tribute to the illustrious master, may be entrusted to conduct us to Bayreuth. We could scarcely ask for a more competent guide:

"This little town . . . which the caprice of a man of genius suddenly made famous, is hidden behind the cool mountain ranges of upper Franconia: pine woods, rapid streams, vast meadows bounded by hills showing faintly blue against a misty sky; long roads bordered with poplars, along which teams of oxen plod slowly, two by two, straining under the copper yokes

that almost form a crown for their heads:—
such are the first impressions as we approach
this town that is ordinarily so peaceful; and
then suddenly, when the theater standing simply and proudly upon the hill has opened its
doors, the same town witnesses a gathering of
emperors, kings and princes from all lands, an
influx of rejoicing crowds, whom the inn-keepers, roused out of their long lethargy, proceed
to plunder to the best of their ability."

The theater, situated outside of the town
and overlooking it, is a structure of simple aspect, somewhat resembling the Trocadéro. In
the interior there are neither boxes nor balconies. The rows of seats form a segment of a
circle of very slight curvature, there are no side
seats, there is no prompter's box, and the orchestra is hidden from view beneath the stage.
Such, in Wagner's eyes, was the way that
drama should be given; and it may well be
asked why we have not followed so good an
example. The parterre contains fifteen hundred seats, and the "Fürstengalerie" two hun-

dred. The stage alone is lighted. Trumpets announce the commencement of each act.

Mme. Judith Gautier has also described Wagner's house, which was built after his own plans. It stands at the end of a broad alley; it is almost square, and is built of reddish gray stone, with no ornamentation excepting a fresco over the front entrance, representing a scene from the *Ring*.

A straight staircase leads to a little antechamber, from which one enters a well lighted and lofty vestibule; it contains a gallery on a level with the second story; it has a marble floor and contains a number of marble statues; to the right is the dining-room, to the left a drawing-room filled with works of art; at the back is a sort of vast library terminating in a rotunda.

Mme. Judith Gautier paid a last visit to Wagner on September 29th, 1881. After crossing the garden, planted with ampelopsis and jars of Bengal roses, and passing a two-story pavilion, a children's gymnasium and a poultry-house, in which she saw peacocks and silver pheasants, she found the master, who welcomed his visitors "with that tremulous eagerness that he always showed to those faithful friends whose love, he felt, was of the perfect sort; for Wagner had no taint of that egotistical indifference that so often affects great men when they have arrived at a certain degree of glory."

Wagner, on this occasion, seemed to be full of gayety and good spirits; and although he spoke French with some difficulty, this fact did not prevent him from indulging in puns and witticisms. He said that he was homesick for sunshine, he wanted to visit India and the Bosphorus. He took his friends to the studio of the artist Joukowski, and then to call upon the machinist Brandt. He talked enthusiastically of his own work.

"When one is young," he said, "when the nerves are not yet wearied, and one can still write opera scores with a certain nimbleness (even that of *Lohengrin*), even if one does not know all the resources of tonal coloring and orchestration, the work is not to be compared with the labor demanded by new works that have to be written in ripe old age. Auber, however, continued to compose up to the age of eighty-four without fatigue, but then he had not changed his manner."

At sixty-nine years of age, Wagner was still capable of considerable activity; he rose at six o'clock; after his bath, he lay down again, and read until ten; at eleven he set to work and continued until two. After dinner he rested again for a short time, reading as before; from four until six he took a carriage ride, after which he resumed his work until eight, spending the rest of the evening with his family. He was a vegetarian by choice. He was patriotic. He was the declared enemy of vivisection, and we know that he always had a great fondness for animals.

"Our campaign," he said to his guests, "has already borne good results in Germany. The carpenters who make the instruments of torture intended for unhappy dogs complain that they do not sell nearly as many."

After all the storms and struggles, Richard Wagner still retained his keen and ardent sensibility. On the occasion of his seventieth anniversary, when a benefit performance was given for the aid of needy musicians, he declared that he was one of them, since he had the most urgent need—of affection! Up to the very end of his life he continued to show the same alternations between violence and singular tenderness.

The spirit of religious reverence which animates his magnificent *Parsifal* also inspires his essay on *Religion and Art*.

After 1879 Wagner was in the habit of passing his winters in Italy. On the thirteenth of February, 1883, he died suddenly in Venice, where he had formerly written *Tristan*, stricken down while at work by apoplexy.

On the evening of his death, his gondolier was found weeping bitterly, on the steps of the Vendramini Palace, where he resided and in

# FROM DREAM TO REALITY 131

which he had a bedroom hung in pale blue and rose-colored satin.

Ludwig II of Bavaria gave orders that no one should touch the body until after the arrival of his envoy. The body was embalmed by Professor Hofmann of Berlin. The king's secretary escorted the remains to the frontier, and in Munich his adjutant general brought a wreath of laurels and palms, with this inscription: "King Ludwig of Bavaria to the great poet of word and music, Richard Wagner."

Wagner was interred in the Villa Wahnfried with great pomp. It required three wagons to carry the wreaths, of which there were more than two hundred.

Ludwig II came next day to weep alone beside his tomb.

Wagner left no fortune at his death, in spite of the fact that the publishing house of Schott, in Mayence, had purchased his score of *Parsifal* for a sum amounting to sixty thousand dollars. His works and his memory are faithfully defended by his widow and his partizans.

He created a human and a superhuman world, which survives him and which transmits his harmonious and richly colored vision of nature and life to all succeeding generations. Accordingly, his long martyrdom, which preceded the far too brief hours of his apotheosis at Bayreuth, was not endured in vain. Has not Wagner himself said that he gave birth in the midst of suffering? This suffering is perpetuated in his majestic works, and is illumined by the rays of love and faith. Thus, the Wagnerian religion was born of his own religion; it fortifies and consoles men today as it fortified and consoled Richard Wagner during his life, a life dedicated to all the infernos and all the glories of immortal art.

PART SECOND

THE WAGNERIAN DRAMA

# CHAPTER I

## SOME PRINCIPLES OF WAGNERIAN ART—POETRY AND MUSIC—FROM OPERA TO DRAMA

A WORK of art, says Richard Wagner, "is religion rendered perceptible in a living form." This definition is, at the same time, the definition of Wagnerian drama.

Brought up among actors, a poet himself from childhood, drawing his inspiration from the lofty conceptions of the Greek tragedians and from Shakespeare, and nurtured on Wieland, Schiller and Goethe, Wagner formed the dream of incorporating music in the drama, and he succeeded perfectly in realizing it.

On the other hand, believing that art was able to convey spiritual truths through physical sensations, he was convinced, as Mr. Chamberlain has ably demonstrated, of the moral significance of the world, and placed his mighty genius for symphonic construction at the service of a philosophy of love and pity and human and religious renovation, or, for the sake of using the consecrated term, redemption.

Now that we have drawn his portrait and followed the essential vicissitudes of his career, it seems worth while to examine briefly his principal characteristics as poet, dramatist and musician, not to say metaphysician.

The poet in him holds considerable place. There have too often been attempts to ignore this, and, besides, his fame as a composer overshadowed that of poet. Are we not in the habit of contemplating people, and famous men are no exception, from a single angle? This is a wide-spread error, and it is all the more serious when the person in question is a Wagner, whose art is essentially a synthetic art composed of the most diverse elements.

Wagner left nothing to chance in his work, which was the fruit of flawless genius and of a prodigiously daring and tenacious will. He wrote all his own librettos, in order that they should be adapted to his music, and in writing them he revealed himself as a delicate and impassioned poet. Berlioz also worked upon his own librettos, but with various collaborators. Wagner adhered invariably to his system. And therein lay his power and his safety.

How many musicians of talent and genius have struggled to infuse life and harmony into shapeless scenarios, mediocre and silly librettos! Beethoven, for whom Wagner professed a keen admiration, amounting almost to a cult, found himself embarrassed by the libretto of *Fidelio*, and was unable to do himself full justice in that opera. As has been convincingly shown by Alfred Ernst, Wagner succeeded in attaining a perfect fusion between the poetic and the musical element.

As a poet, Wagner was master of his forms even in his earliest productions; he drew his inspiration from ancient texts, he employed both regular rhyme and alliteration, he revived archaic terms, and excelled, especially in *Tris-*

*tan and Isolde,* in coining new substances of broad significance.

If the composition of the *Ring of the Nibelung* is the work of a master, the poem of *Tannhäuser* is in itself a profound inspiration, exquisite in sentiment, the work of a writer possessed at once of great vigor and great charm. The famous *Romance of the Star* and the *Invocation of Venus* are poems which would do honor to the best poets of contemporary Germany.

Similarly, the rhythms and cadences in *Parsifal* prove him to be an artist of exquisite subtlety in the value of words. It is certain that when such ingenious and discerning writers as Gérard de Nerval, Baudelaire, and Villiers de l'Isle Adam made themselves heralds of the Wagnerian drama, they had an intuitive perception not only of his vast purposes, but of the lyric audacity and wealth of poetic resources that are so easily to be found in him.

Accordingly, Wagner is a great poet, and it should be at once added, a great dramatic poet.

## WAGNERIAN ART 139

As a dramatist, he could not limit his genius within the bounds of recorded history. Wagner did not become himself until subsequently to *Rienzi*. He could move at ease in the midst of immense, mysterious subjects, among legends and myths, in which the characters, while making us feel their kinship, have no difficulty in taking on the quality of heroes and divinities. Invention and fantasy are not only permissible but even necessary to themes of this character. In their primitive form they already contain symbols; transmitted from generation to generation, they become the embodiment of the soul of a people, and hence lend themselves to the original symbolism of the modern artist.

The Wagnerian drama, contained in three acts, which carry us from the exposition to the dénouement, through all the fluctuations of the plot, transports us to fairyland by its swift changes of scene and more especially by the pomp and diversity of its spectacles.

And as such, it is no longer content to be merely a drama, but becomes a sort of festival, majestic, national, religious. And why should we be surprised at the luxury and prodigality of Richard Wagner, when we remember his concrete love of sumptuous, amazing, dazzling decorations? Such, for example, as the storm in the *Rhinegold*, followed by the rainbow; or again the Rhine-Maidens, depicting nature in her strangest and most fascinating aspects.

In the midst of these enchanted settings, his personages are exalted, his characters rise above human desire and heroic will to the heights of abnegation and renouncement. Thus it is that we have side by side, Elsa and Isolde, Brunnhilde and Kundry, Wolfram and Lohengrin, Siegfried and Parsifal. Earthly passions join hands with celestial sacrifices.

In order to realize of what great variety Wagner is capable in his creation of characters, it will suffice to compare the daring Siegfried with the crafty dwarf Mime, and to contrast the good and adroit Hans Sachs in the *Meistersinger*, with the sorrowing and divine Tristan.

Is it true that Richard Wagner availed himself of existing and fully developed types, contenting himself with placing them in a setting of musical tragedy? In order to convince ourselves of the contrary, it will be sufficient to consider the differences pointed out by Albert Ernst, between the Scandinavian Odin and the Wotan of the Tetralogy.

Wagner's mysticism which, in our opinion, has set in motion throughout the length and breadth of Europe a current of ideas and sentiments in opposition to the doctrine of positivism, found free scope in this atmosphere of miracles, magic and damnation. And it is the Christian idea of sacrifice which asserts itself all the way from the *Flying Dutchman* to *Parsifal*. More than that, as has not failed to be noticed on numerous occasions, Christianity is, in certain cases, contrasted with paganism. For instance, in *Tannhäuser*, Venus vanishes when the name of Mary is uttered.

As for *Parsifal*, it is a veritable mystery play, and the triumph of religious feeling in this last of Wagner's works has been generally recognized. It is certain, nevertheless, that Wagner intended it, not as an apology for any particular sect, but as a magnificent affirmation of pure evangelism.

Amid all the confusing mass of dissertations and discussions, involving all degrees of Wagnerianism, it seemed necessary to try to get a clear conception of his general tendencies. Now that we have done so, it remains to ask, what are the laws which govern his musical drama?

They become more and more defined, in proportion as he departs from conventional opera and develops his own method with a majestic amplitude that is sometimes complex to the point of obscurity. It is above all in the *Meistersinger* and *Tristan*, or in *Parsifal*, that we may study his system and compare it with the accepted methods of the opera.

In the true Wagnerian musical drama, we no longer have recitatif, no isolated lyrics with their required rhythms. The characters carry on a dialogue, there is an orchestral movement accompanying the action. The orchestra expresses and generalizes all the emotions, analyzing them to the utmost fugitive shading; and the critics have good reason for drawing a comparison with the rôle played by the chorus in Greek tragedy when they attempt to define that of the orchestra in the Wagnerian drama. The symphony of motives serves as a description of the elements of nature and of the drama: for instance, the undulation of the waves, and the gallop of the Walkyries.

The prelude permits us to participate in a sort of dream-vision of the action of the drama, and consists of an idealized commentary on the events we are about to witness. It is a collective and powerfully suggestive meditation, a harmonious philosophizing over the persons and the events which the musician is about to conjure up.

It is generally known, furthermore, that in each drama there are a number of leading themes of leitmotiv consisting of basic melodies. Gluck, to be sure, had already employed this method. Wagner certainly did not invent it. Beethoven utilized it, and so did Mozart. But Wagner built up his works on a foundation of these characteristic themes.

With him, the melody accompanies the action and never recurs arbitrarily. The themes employed undergo a multitude of variations, distinguished from one another as a result of successive modifications. This is perfectly logical. An individual remains himself, even when he alters; and it is the same way with everything that is human, everything that forms part of the universe and is in a perpetual state of change.

In spite of the extreme complexity of certain of these themes, it has been observed that this tempestuous revolutionist never went to extremes, in regard to the vocal difficulties of his rôles. But he needed experienced actors, with a gift for mobile and expressive mimicry. His singers have to play and to make use of all their means. Wagner demands of each one all that he can give, in the same way that he himself exhausts all the combinations in the development and analysis of a passion that has become a musical element.

Wagner's harmony unites the traditional counterpoint of the schools with the independent development of melodies. Whatever may constitute the striking originality of the author of the *Tetralogy,* his work is not an isolated and unforeseen phenomenon, but it carries on, in a gigantic synthesis, on the one hand the work of Gluck, and on the other that of Bach and Beethoven.

Thanks to the innumerable resources of his orchestra, he succeeds in giving a strong and vivid personality even to the minor characters in his dramas. The instruments are apportioned in groups, and reunited in families; each one has its own particular rôle. It has been remarked, for instance, that while, in the *Ring of the Nibelung,* the tuba-counterbass indicates in a certain way the redoubtable personality of the giant Fafner, the trombone-counterbass indicates that of Wotan, and announces his profound and dominating voice. We know how many sentiments Wagner has succeeded in expressing in his music-language, enormous and tumultuous, eloquent and tender, thanks to the horns and the clarinets.

But let us leave to technical musicians the care of studying in detail and with precision the Wagnerian methods of expression, and, if they choose, his habitual processes, which became more and more defined as he attained full self-mastery. We will not even stop to ask whether his rules have not done harm to some over-zealous disciples, and hampered the full expansion of certain musical personalities.

## CHAPTER II

**THE GREAT WAGNERIAN THEMES—FROM LOVE TO SACRIFICE—IN THE REALM OF DREAMS AND BEAUTY**

ONE of the most authoritative interpreters of Wagner's works and doctrines, Mr. Chamberlain, has said that the first of Wagner's operas, *The Fairies* (1833), which was produced in Munich some years after the master's death, in June, 1888, contained "something quite prophetic," not only in some of its musical developments, but also in the theme, in which the plot is subordinate and the idea of redemption is sharply emphasized.

But this work survives only as an indication and a curiosity.

Although the *Liebesverbot*, or *Novice of Palermo*, contains a melody afterwards introduced into *Tannhäuser* (the Pardon of the Pilgrims), it is of very slight significance. The libretto is a veritable imbroglio that reminds one of certain old stock comedies, crowded with hackneyed episodes such as disguises, abductions, a confused mass of intrigues, letters, exits, entrances, etc.

The work, however, is interesting for two reasons: in the first place, because of the doubled fervor of poet and musician, which reveals a curious and poignant sense of the picturesque; and secondly, because it represents a state of mind. Young Wagner, thirsting for liberty, an enemy of traditional German operatic music, here shows himself equally the enemy of puritanical hypocrisy. He exalts pleasures and passions.

*Rienzi,* or *The Last of the Tribunes,* is a conventional opera, destined primarily for the Grand Opéra at Paris, drawing its inspiration from the customs of the period, and resembling the works of Halévy, Scribe and Meyerbeer. It is an historic drama, with far too much history in it, overburdened with detail and constantly

## GREAT WAGNERIAN THEMES 149

sacrificing the development of the spiritual conflicts expressed by the musical motives, to purely human action.

The scenic effects are adroitly managed, and the score is not lacking in color nor in strength. Indeed, this strength is carried to the point of brutality. We realize this while listening to the overture, which is none the less full of admirable qualities. Wagner himself was the first to see his mistakes, the first to realize what his score lacked; and he underwent a reaction, not only against the other contemporary musicians but against himself. The *Flying Dutchman,* produced only a few months later than *Rienzi,* is the manifest and brilliant proof of this.

Here we are in the presence of Wagnerian drama in its first phase, with those leitmotivs (the importance of which, as M. J. G. Prud'homme has very justly observed, Berlioz had already recognized in his *Fantastique*), with its symphonic orchestration, with its suppression of all useless diversions tending to interrupt the dramatic action, with what was then considered the daring freedom of its soaring harmonies, and the especially bold employment of chromatic scales. With the *Flying Dutchman,* Wagner's rupture with conventional opera was accomplished. By emancipating himself from an illogical form, he was henceforth free to work in a manner congenial to his temperament.

Furthermore, he had not only found his system, but he had also discovered a type of subjects that would permit him to expound the human and divine themes of love, anguish, pity and regeneration. The theme of the *Flying Dutchman,* and the motive of redemption, which is superbly developed in Senta's ballad, are most significant in this regard. Moreover, the popular legend of the *Accursed Dutchman* was peculiarly calculated to appeal to the melancholy nature of that other wandering and ill-fated soul, the tempestuous, sorrowful and romantic Richard Wagner.

He gave a new and deeper color to the original version of the legend by his own splendid aspirations, which gave a vibrant intensity to the marvelous prologue to the *Flying Dutchman,* and to the score of the opera itself, which, although uneven, is full of vigor and of a lofty and touching psychology. For in this work Wagner no longer wasted his time in binding together a series of episodes, and describing them by external methods. One would say rather, that he had concentrated his attention on the human soul, with all that it contained of pathetic nostalgia and helpless yearning, and had magnified its quivering pulsations. In doing this he left the domain of history and time, and in a certain sense spiritualized his inspiration. Wagner was yet destined to become the sonorous echo of those secret religious inquietudes concealed in the inmost depths of the noblest souls.

The theme of the *Flying Dutchman,* imbued as it is with a spirit of wild and somber poetry, was well adapted to the development of Wagnerian symbolism. The unfortunate victim of the malediction cannot be saved unless through the tender devotion of a woman. Let us not inquire too closely why Senta, the daughter of Daland, falls in love, in advance, with the accursed stranger. Let us yield ourselves to the mystery within the mystery. Insensible to the passion of Erik the hunter, Senta has yielded her heart to an ideal love. When the Hollander reaches shore, she recognizes him as the one whose salvation she is destined to accomplish through the purity of her love. She will follow him and give herself to him. When the vessel prepares to depart in the midst of a tempest, she ascends a rock and flings herself into the waves, in order to reach the victim of the curse. The sea engulfs the vessel, but love, stronger than death, will unite Senta to him whom she has redeemed, in celestial beatitudes.

Under similar circumstances, Elizabeth sacrifices herself to the knight *Tannhäuser*, in the romantic opera in three acts which bears his name, and which is the outgrowth of a popular legend and of the war of the singers of the Wartburg.

In spite of his numerous experiments with foreign themes, Wagner, from his youth up, was theoretically in favor of a national drama, capable of thrilling the heart of the entire nation. It must not be forgotten that it was Weber's *Freischütz* which first awakened his artistic sensibility and revealed to him the mission of which he was destined little by little to acquire a clearer and more profound conception.

Now, *Tannhäuser* furnished him with a theme typical of old Germany—romantic, chivalrous and idealistic. At the same time, the conflict between the senses and the soul, between Venus and the Divine Spirit, underlies the legend and gives it its human and universal significance. In the seductive and picturesque personage of Tannhäuser the mad, unbridled desire for pleasure is at war with the immaculate glory of eternal salvation. The conception of pagan ebriety, which Nietzsche has undertaken to exalt in all his works, here blends with the ethereal hymn of Christian ecstasies.

It is this two-fold and powerful inspiration that animates the magnificent Overture, wherein we see reflected a generalization of the entire drama, and which later animates the drama itself.

The young and venturous knight, Tannhäuser, like Goethe's Faust, is in search of happiness. Amidst nymphs and bacchantes, in Venus's grotto and at her feet, he savors voluptuous joys; indeed, he has savored them too long, since he has wearied of the intoxication of the unbridled senses. That is why his troubled soul is anxious to escape from the Venusberg and return to its share of earthly trials. But the goddess and her sirens hold him by their seductive power. The hero wishes to break this charm, and when Venus curses him, he invokes the sacred name of Mary. Venus vanishes, and the hero returns to the smiling valley of the Wartburg and to the common life of men.

We are back in the heart of the Middle Ages, in old Thuringia, amid the songs of pilgrims and shepherds. The Landgrave, surrounded by his poet-knights, has gone hunting. "Return among us and mingle your voice with ours," his noble rival and friend Wolfram says to Tannhäuser. And faithful friendship pours itself out in song in the andante of the sextette which urges him to return and take his place among his peers. Tannhäuser hesitates. But when Wolfram speaks of the Landgrave's niece, Elizabeth, who still loves him, he decides to accompany them. Everyone knows the allegro, the stretto of which is interrupted by the hunting horns at the close of the first act of *Tannhäuser*.

Now we are at the Wartburg. Even down to the present time it has retained its medieval aspect, and the chamber is still exhibited where Luther threw the ink-bottle at the devil. But to return to *Tannhäuser:* conducted by the loyal Wolfram, he throws himself at Elizabeth's feet. Then ensues a sublime love duet, in the course of which the knight pours forth his yearning for infinite ecstasy. Accompanied by his singers, the Landgrave proposes, at this juncture, a singing contest, in which love is to be worthily celebrated in the presence of the lords and noble ladies. Wolfram, who also loves Elizabeth, glorifies his sentiments with equal amplitude and discretion. Tannhäuser responds. Little by little, he yields to the magic spell of his memories, and exalts burning passion and the intoxications known only to those who have penetrated the Venusberg.

This pagan invocation horrifies his audience. The knights wish to kill the author of such a scandal, but Elizabeth saves him, for she loves him in spite of all. . . . And it is decided that Tannhäuser shall accompany the pilgrims to Rome, in order to sue for pardon.

Elizabeth patiently awaits the return of the one to whom she has given her heart and whom she has pardoned in advance. But Tannhäuser is not to be found among the returning pilgrims. The tender and fair Elizabeth prays for his salvation. Wolfram, in the dim dawn of day, sings his famous *Romance of the Star*, and Tannhäuser advances. He has failed to obtain his pardon. With bitter sarcasm he tells the tale of his journey. At all events, he will find intoxication and forgetfulness with Venus, and the nymphs and sirens whom he invokes.

Venus who has come at his summons, once more vanishes. A mournful procession escorts the body of the unfortunate Elizabeth, who has been unable to survive her grief. The knight Tannhäuser finds pure and ideal love as he dies beside his beloved, and he will be reunited to her in the realm of grace and eternity.

In *Tannhäuser*, notwithstanding its dream atmosphere, Wagner could not rid himself of certain obligations towards recorded history. *Lohengrin*, however, the Knight of the Swan, which he borrowed from the legend of the

Graal, that was destined also to furnish him *Parsifal,* left full liberty to his imagination and fantasy.

It is an exquisite conception, and very general in its symbolism. Wagner himself compared it to the story of Jupiter and Semele, and said further:

"The type of Lohengrin appealed to me with a constantly increasing power of attraction. . . . I learned to understand the myth of *Lohengrin* in its simplest significance, that is to say, in its most profound significance as a truly popular poem. . . . *Lohengrin* is by no means exclusively the product of a Christian conception."

It is certain, none the less, that the seraphic knight owes a great deal to "Christian conception," whatever may have been Wagner's opinion.

The legend is familiar: it is charming, enigmatic, and poignantly poetic.

The king of Germany, Henry the Falconer, holds plenary court on the banks of the

## GREAT WAGNERIAN THEMES 159

Scheldt. Count Telramund, at the instigation of his wife, brings a charge against Elsa, Princess of Brabant, falsely accusing her of having killed her brother, the heir to the throne. They proceed to the trial by combat. If no knight offers himself as Elsa's champion, she is lost. And it seems likely that she will be, since no one comes forward to defend her cause. She prays and supplicates, but in vain. Then, suddenly, a Swan appears, drawing a little boat, whose occupant is the knight of dreams and mystery who is destined to save Elsa. He defeats Telramund in combat, but spares his life. Elsa is to become his wife. But first she must promise that she will never ask to know the name of the Knight of the Swan.

The wedding takes place. Elsa is tender and loving; but she is a woman, which means that she is curious. It should be added that the wicked Ortrude arouses painful doubts in her mind. In the nuptial chamber, after soft avowals, Elsa forgets her promise and begs to know where her noble savior and husband has come from. At this moment, Telramund enters, hoping to take the knight unaware, but the latter kills him. Elsa faints; curiosity has extinguished love.

When Lohengrin has revealed his name, which is that of the son of the knight Parsifal, king of the Graal, and his mission, which is to defend innocence, he is obliged, in obedience to his oath, to disappear. The Swan returns and Lohengrin departs; we see him fading into the distance. He has gone. It is in vain that Elsa moans and laments. He no longer exists for her; in her despair she falls lifeless; doubt has killed love and happiness.

If the drama properly so called lacks the proportions and the interest of *Tannhäuser*, *Lohengrin* because of its sustained style and magnificent perfection remains the evocation of a melancholy and enchanting dream.

Liszt, to whom Wagner's fame owes so large a debt, has expressed his appreciation of the music of *Lohengrin* in the highest terms. It is, he says, the ideal of synthetic art. "Its princi-

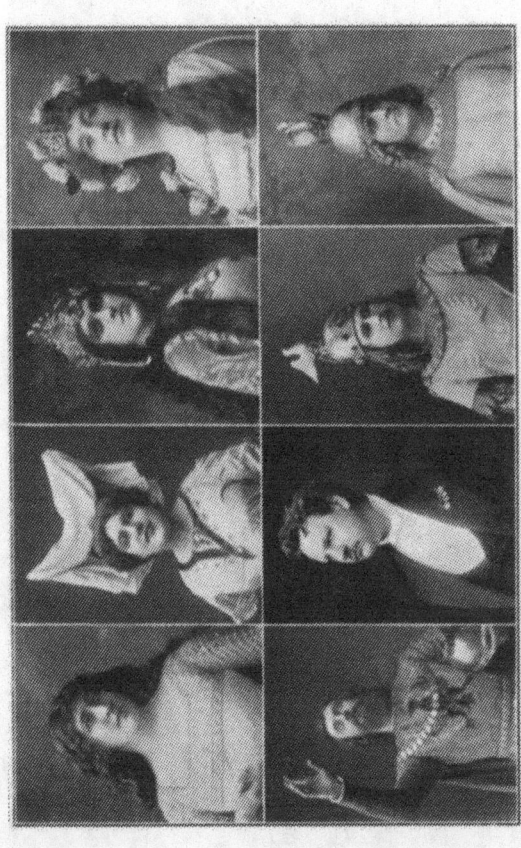

THE PRINCIPAL INTERPRETERS OF WAGNER IN AMERICA
Mmes. Gadski, Destinn, Ober, Fornia. Messrs. Witherspoon, Slezak, Urlus and Kingston

## GREAT WAGNERIAN THEMES 161

pal characteristic is such perfect unity of conception and style that not a phrase nor an ensemble nor a passage of any sort whatever can be found which, if separated from the work as a whole, could be understood in its true sense and definite character."

We feel that henceforth Wagner is sure of himself, and of his musical resources; they are revealed more plainly and definitively in his wonderful *Tristan,* to write which he interrupted the composition of his Tetralogy.

After the separation which followed their noble and melancholy renouncement, Wagner wrote from Venice to Mathilde Wesendonck, in reference to *Tristan and Isolde,* which was the embodiment of all his despair and all his longing to find consolation in his mystic art:

"What music this is going to be! Never until now have I done anything to equal it!"

And from Zurich, he wrote again to the same friend:

"When *Tristan* is finished, it seems to me that a marvelous period of my life will have been brought to a close, and that I shall be able henceforth to gaze upon the world peacefully, clearly, profoundly, with a new-born soul."

Accordingly, *Tristan and Isolde*, taken chiefly from the German poem of Gottfried of Strassburg, must be thought of as reborn from the love and sorrow of the great romantic poet. As Henri Lichtenberger has well said, the lament of Tristan, tortured by desire and stretching out his arms towards beneficent night and the torches of kindly death, gushed straight from Wagner's very heart.

In glorifying an unforgettable love, the musician surpassed himself. After he was cured of his attack of Wagnerianism, Nietzsche, even in the very act of flaying the friend whom he had formerly adored, could not prevent himself from exclaiming:

"The world must seem a very poor place to anyone who has never been ill enough to appreciate that inferno of passionate love."

Evidently, the whole power of the work lies in its effusion, its pessimism, its fever of anni-

## GREAT WAGNERIAN THEMES 163

hilation, and Buddhism. We know how strongly the doctrine of Nirvana, revived by Schopenhauer, had impressed Wagner during his residence at Zurich. Love and death are the great themes of this drama, and the prelude celebrates them with extraordinary amplitude.

Isolde, princess of Ireland, is betrothed, against her will, but in conformity with a treaty between the two countries, to the king of Cornwall, Mark. We first see her on board the ship that is bearing her to this sad union. Consequently she is praying for death. The nephew of the king, the peerless knight Tristan, is in command of the ship. He is grave and preoccupied. He and Isolde are united in a passion which bursts out of bounds when they drink from a cup into which a love philter has been poured. They are still lost in a mad whirl of emotion when the ship reaches the realm of King Mark.

After an interval of suspense the lovers are reunited in a night of love and ecstasy. Their hymn rises and swells, sublime, unlimited, exalted by the harps, and it blends with the motives of glorification and of death. The king surprises them. Why has Tristan betrayed him? And Tristan, begging Isolde to follow across the dark river, allows himself to be wounded. He has risen to the height of renunciation, to the sacrifice of death.

We are now transferred to Tristan's own castle, where he lies ill, dying amid somber harmonies. The plaintive air of the shepherd's pipe blends with Tristan's dying agony. The faithful Isolde comes to join him on the coast of Brittany, but when she reaches him, he is dead, and she too has come there only to die. The arrival of King Mark, the punishment of Melot, the death of the loyal Kurwenal are all crowded together in the third act for the purpose of accentuating the sacrifice of Isolde, who dies in ecstasy because she is going to be united to Tristan through all eternity.

It was in Paris, after the fiasco of *Tannhäuser*, that Wagner set to work upon the text of the *Meistersinger*.

"It is certainly funny," he wrote to his wife, Minna, "that I should be working here on my Master Singers of Nuremberg, and looking out on the Tuileries and the Louvre. I cannot help laughing heartily, many a time, when I look out of the window."

The *Meistersinger* occupies a position by itself among Wagner's works, and it is by no means the smallest jewel in his crown. It is a joyous and radiant satire upon official and conventional æsthetics, and at the same time a humorous piece of special pleading *pro domo;* in a series of comic and ironical situations, it pictures the apotheosis of the genius of an artist who soars to his full height when brought in contact with the genius of his race.

Accordingly, the *Meistersinger* is a sort of musical comedy, but in its technique, as well as in the loftiness of its sentiments, combined with the portrayal of burlesque characters, it is an original work of distinct importance and real power. In this work, Wagner's distinctive manner is revealed in its full perfection.

The young knight, Walther von Stolzing, has come from Franconia to Nuremberg. He is in love with the charming Eva, daughter of the opulent goldsmith, Pogner. Walther,—we almost wrote "Wagner," and probably with good reason,—decides to compete for the grade of master in the singers' guild of that city. His brave and noble inspiration refuses to be fettered by sterile rules. The town clerk, Beckmesser, is his ridiculous rival.

As night approaches, Walther prepares to elope with Eva. But he is prevented by chance events, such as the passing by of the town watchman and the grotesque serenade by Beckmesser. Fortunately the kind-hearted and worthy Hans Sachs, the poet-cobbler, has undertaken to defend Walther. It is thanks to his cleverness and far-sighted sagacity that Walther converts both the master-singers and the people, and wins his happiness.

The character of Hans Sachs, with his hidden sorrow,—for he has cast a wistful glance at Eva before coming to the aid of the lovers

# GREAT WAGNERIAN THEMES 167

and working devotedly for their union, compels our admiration, equally with his delightful revery beneath the lilacs, on St. John's eve.

The much lamented Alfred Ernst was quite justified in seeing in the marriage of the young knight Walther, representative of an exclusive caste, with Eva, daughter of the people, the fruitful union of noble art and popular inspiration. But quite aside from this happy symbolism, one cannot help being charmed with the series of typical songs so picturesquely interspersed among the leitmotivs. The composition of the work, showing exceptional abundance and vigor, unites scholastic forms with the most minute details of an "advanced" technique. It sets us thinking of Bach, and then it sets us thinking of . . . none else than Wagner himself, in the full splendor of his polyphonic utterance.

## CHAPTER III

EPIC AND LYRIC—FROM HUMAN DEITIES TO
DIVINE HUMANITY—A GOSPEL IN MUSIC

RICHARD WAGNER, the Æschylus of modern times, has written a vast tragic epic, in which he has undertaken, in the course of a gigantic action, human and divine, to examine the problem of destinies and the continuous development of the passions, interpreted by words and music intimately blended in a universal drama.

Such is his *Ring of the Nibelung,* piously dedicated to King Ludwig II of Bavaria.

The Tetralogy consists of a prologue, called the *Rhinegold,* and three day-long episodes.

After listening to the leitmotiv of nature, the great cosmogonic theme of the work, and after meditating upon the forces of the uni-

## A GOSPEL IN MUSIC 169

verse, distributed among all animate and inanimate things, we see the daughters of the Rhine, Woglinde, Wellgunde, and Flosshilde. The Nibelung, Alberich, drawn hither by desire, learns that whoever possesses himself of the river's gold and forges the magic ring, will obtain dominion over the universe. Ambition holds sovereign sway over the soul of Alberich, who snatches the gold of the Rhine. He has renounced love. The desire for power has entered into him.

Walhalla, the abode of the gods, next appears to us, and there we find Wotan, king of the gods, and his wife Fricka. Wotan has promised Freia, goddess of youth and beauty, to the giants Fasolt and Fafner, who come to claim her. Through Loge, the fire-god, it is learned that the Nibelung, Alberich, has stolen the gold of the Rhine. Wotan, in his turn, relinquishes love along with Freia, for the sake of obtaining the gold. The giants depart, taking Freia with them. All nature becomes darkened. Loge, the flame which flickers here and there, advises Wotan to follow him to the Nibelung's forge.

From the stolen gold, Alberich has had made Tarnhelm, the helmet that renders its wearer invisible, the sword Nothung, and the ring which renders its possessor master of the universe. The astute Loge flatters the dwarf Alberich and asks him whether it is true that he can assume at will the form of any animal whatever. Alberich metamorphoses himself into a dragon, and then into a toad.

He is seized and fettered. Finding himself a prisoner, Alberich consents to yield up his treasures, hoping that he can keep the ring. But Wotan snatches it from him. Vanquished, the Nibelung utters the baleful malediction of the ring which is destined to overhang all the personages in the trilogy.

Warned by the primeval mother of all beings, Erda, soul of the world, Wotan yields the ring to the giants who have brought back Freia. The giants quarrel. Fafner kills Fasolt with a blow from a club. The gods triumph as the

# A GOSPEL IN MUSIC 171

sky clears. The appearance of a rainbow succeeds the tumult of the storm. The gods return, two by two, to the motiv of Walhalla. But the daughters of the Rhine lament and will continue to lament so long as the sparkle of the gold is missing from the waters of the Rhine. Who will pay the penalty for the crime? Who will be the redeemer? Wotan ponders as he hears the clarion notes of the sword motiv.

It should be noted that all the motivs of the triple drama here appear in their first bare simplicity.

We have lived with the gods; now we are going to live chiefly with heroes.

As we follow in thought the noble prelude of the *Walkyrie,* the admirable language of the double basses and violoncellos, and the motiv of the Magic fire begun by the bass tubas, and taken up by the trombones and cornets, we must needs know or remember that Wotan, having become the God-wolf, hunted by dogs, begot twins, Siegmund and Sieglinde. From his union with Erda he had his favorite daughter, Brunnhilde; she has been brought up with the Walkyries, whose function is to receive the souls of heroes, in order to transport them to Walhalla.

We are now in the presence of a barbarous stage of humanity, but nearer to reality than what has gone before. In a cabin in the depths of the forest dwells Sieglinde; here she receives a stranger clad in the skins of beasts; it is Siegmund. She is the wife of Hunding, who is of the race of hunters, while Siegmund belongs to the race of wolves. Nevertheless, Hundling respects the laws of hospitality, since his enemy is his guest. Siegmund sleeps and dreams of the sword which will give him dominion. Sieglinde comes to him and shows where the promised sword is hidden. The pair confess their love, in a glorification of youth and spring-time.

The incestuous love between brother and sister has not failed to give bitter offense. But are we not in the realm of myth and legend, almost apart from time and space? Far from resenting this idyll of Siegmund and Sieglinde, who seeks to be saved from the dog, Hunding, one Wagnerian critic has lauded the beauty of the symbolism; a god incarnated in his children in order to atone for his own sin, and then compelled himself to decree their death and to see every hope of salvation die with them.

Wotan is gloomy; his ancient sin will not be expiated until the gold is returned to the daughters of the Rhine. Now, it is the will of destiny that Siegmund shall not be the savior; he is not the looked-for hero. He is destined to fall under the blows of the hunter Hunding. This is what Wotan announces to his daughter, the Valkyrie, and his words give the key to the drama:

"Announce to the hero Siegmund," he tells her, "that this evening he will enter into Walhalla! For the purpose of begetting a son who should be the savior of the divine race, I have wandered upon earth, I have become a beast of the woods, a wolf-god hunted by dogs.

Yet today my son Siegmund, who, armed with the sword, was to have returned the gold to the daughters of the Rhine and expiated the sin for which I am torn with remorse, Siegmund, alas, must die!"

Brunnhilde appears to Siegmund, who is fleeing through the solitudes, accompanied by Sieglinde. The Valkyrie announces his destiny to him, but on beholding the affection of the pair for each other, Brunnhilde is stirred to pity. Accordingly, when the duel takes place, she herself turns aside Hunding's sword with her silver shield. Hereupon Wotan, who is the instrument of highest Destiny, breaks Siegmund's sword with his own all powerful spear, and Siegmund is pierced through the heart. Then follows the cavalcade of the Valkyries, with their clamors, their songs, their furious stampede.

Brunnhilde saves Sieglinde, who must hide the broken fragments of the sword in the forest. And there in the forest Sieglinde bears a son to the dead hero, who is ordained by the fates to achieve the salvation of the gods. The motiv of Siegfried, radiant and victorious, informs us of this hope.

But the rebellious Brunnhilde must be punished. Wotan himself is obliged to pass sentence on his favorite daughter.

"You shall sleep," the god tells her, "until a man finds you and awakens you, and you shall become his wife."

What humiliation for the proud virgin goddess of Walhalla! But at least let this man be a hero, let her retreat be surrounded with a wall of flame. Wotan, himself in despair, consents, and we witness their leave-taking. The motiv of Brunnhilde's justification is followed by the motiv of sleep in the bosom of nature.

Accordingly, the free and joyous hero, who is destined to recover the ring and to awaken the Valkyrie, is Siegfried, son of Siegmund and Sieglinde. Wotan reveals to us his regrets and his aspirations, and initiates us into the general significance of the work: *Siegfried* is a splendid poem of youth, strong, beautiful, naïve, sincere, unspoiled by civilization, and in full possession of its irresistible and sublime spontaneity.

Siegfried has been brought up by Alberich's brother, the crafty dwarf Mime, who is scheming to avail himself of the youth's courage to destroy the dragon. Then he himself can obtain possession of the ring, and with it universal power. The naïveté of the youth seems to guarantee the success of these dark designs.

Meanwhile, Siegfried welds the broken fragments of the sword Nothung. He is destined to triumph over the craftiness of the dwarf, as well as over the unchained forces of the elements. The symphony of the forest seems to proclaim the grandeur of his destiny. He is the incarnation of new humanity, in the heart of nature. He watches the beasts of the forest, he has inborn powers of domination. The dragon, Fafner, who in spite of flames and smoke fails to alarm us seriously, fails equally to alarm Siegfried. Having slain the dragon, he listens to the bird of the wood, echo of our thoughts, enters Fafner's cave and places the ring upon his finger.

"He alone who has never known fear shall awaken Brunnhilde." Such is the decree of destiny, and Siegfried is the appointed one. Wotan is obliged to allow him to pass, and from that moment foresees the downfall of the gods.

Siegfried advances and penetrates within the circle of flames, and this passage through the fire is expounded by magnificent cadences upon the harp. He discovers a woman asleep, a majestic and supreme revelation of Love and Beauty. And then comes the incomparable awakening of Brunnhilde. She salutes the light of day. She strives to repulse Siegfried, yet she cannot help loving him because of his triumphant youth and strength. Henceforth the gods may perish, since love has been granted her.

Accordingly, the Tetralogy closes with the *Götterdämmerung*, the Twilight of the Gods, which is expounded to us in the prelude. Once again we hear the horn of Siegfried, blending with the motiv of the primeval elements. The hero Siegfried cannot remain inactive. Like the demi-god of Greek mythology, he must accomplish his mission in the world.

The daughters of the Rhine continue to lament. Siegfried, in the course of his wanderings, is received by Gunther and his sister Gutrune, the latter of whom makes him drink the philter of forgetfulness. And in consequence oblivion invades his soul. He asks Gutrune in marriage, and agrees to bring Brunnhilde to be Gunther's bride. In vain Brunnhilde urges her claim upon Siegfried. He is not to remember his love for her until during the hunt, when Hagen makes him drink of a new philter which destroys the effect of the first. Siegfried is relating the story of his youth and his exploits, when he is stricken down by a treacherous blow from Hagen and expires, evoking the memory of Brunnhilde. And the motiv of Siegfried's death seems like the chant of universal mourning. Hagen and

Gunther quarrel over the possession of the ring, when Brunnhilde appears. She consults destiny and must succumb to the ordained fate of death. And she must give back the ring to the daughters of the Rhine. Redemption through love forms the majestic conclusion to this great epic tragedy.

What interpretation are we to give it? Is the *Ring* socialistic, anarchistic, Christian or pessimistic? It seems best to regard the legend as the exposition of eternal ideas and emotions, a summing-up of human attributes and passions, from Siegfried's youthful daring to Wotan's abdication. And above all it is important to recognize it as the embodiment of the Wagnerian system in all its splendor, as well as in its austere and somewhat oppressive complexity. The lyric and dramatic elements are here profoundly intermingled. The theory of the drama, as opposed to the old conventional opera, robbed of all fioritura, consecrated wholly to the exposition, through the blended words and music, of superhuman deeds, is here freely developed, broadly, powerfully, and in definitive manner.

Let us not mar the beauty of this immense myth by abstruse dialectics or vain esoteric commentary, but let us be content to accept it as a sublime song of joy and sorrow magnified by the dreams and the genius of an artist who is also prodigious from the technical point of view. Better than anywhere else, we may follow his method as it is succinctly expounded by Gasperini:

"When Wagner has created a melodic idea, it recurs under a thousand forms, modified by the most delicate processes of modulation, by infinite evolutions of the rhythm, it is developed to a point at which it seems exhausted, it is enriched by unforeseen episodes that suddenly flow forth, it is prolonged in magnificent amplifications, and then little by little it loses its color, is stripped of its sharp characteristics, becomes diluted, melts away, dies out, unrecognizable in one final burst of harmony."

As may well be imagined, the Tetralogy, like

## A GOSPEL IN MUSIC 181

all the rest of Wagner's works, became a target for the humorists. In Germany, quite as much as in France, the spirit of satire expended itself freely upon the *Ring of the Nibelung*. M. Grand-Carteret has shown no little cleverness and erudition in gathering together a collection of these amusing pleasantries. Here, for example, is the manner in which two Berlinese, Schultze and Müller, have simplified the libretto of the *Ring*, in order to reduce it to the dimensions required for a parlor edition,—and heaven knows that parlor gossip usurped the task of attending to Wagner's reputation and defended it with jealous care, especially after it had practically ceased to be attacked!

Seven characters and seven scenes; a spectacle accompanied by full orchestra, playing variations upon the air, "There were seven who wanted a ring."

*Scene 1st*. The Daughters of the Rhine, while dancing in a circle, lose their golden ring. Alberich arrives and takes possession of it, saying, "With your permission!"

*Scene 2d.* Alberich, well satisfied with "what the waves have brought him," ascends to Walhalla; it is already late, and the palace will be shut if he arrives after dark; but suddenly the god Wotan appears and saying politely, "with your permission," takes possession of the ring found on his territory.

*Scene 3d.* Wotan and the giants, who have come to demand either Freia or his treasure. As the god proves somewhat stubborn, they say to him, "We want this ring and we are going to have it!" adding, "with your permission, of course." But since there are two of them, it occurs to Fafner that they cannot both wear one ring, so he forthwith dismisses Fasold into the next world.

*Scene 4th.* Fafner, transformed into a dragon, through fear of thieves, is standing guard over his treasure, when Siegfried arrives.

"Let me tell you, O Fafner, how much your ring pleases me!"

"Be off with you," cries papa Fafner, "or it

will be the worse for you! You can easily find a ring just like it at any jeweler's."

"No, yours is the one I must have."

"Look out, or I will make it hot for you!"

But Siegfried runs the dragon through, and then says politely,

"Now you will have to do as you are told! With your permission!"

*Scene 5th.* Siegfried and Brunnhilde love each other tenderly and are exchanging vows.

"Give me your ring," says Brunnhilde caressingly. "It will look well on my finger, and in exchange I will let you have my horse, Grane. What, do you hesitate? Then you don't love me! Perhaps you are in love with some other girl! I may take it, mayn't I? With your permission?"

*Scene 6th.* "Brunnhilde, give me back that ring!"

And he snatches it from her.

*Scene 7th.* Siegfried is dead, and a certain Hagen has come to steal the ring. But dead though he is, he can still move his ring finger and will not permit the much disputed treasure to be removed from it.

Finally Brunnhilde ascends the funeral pyre beside Siegfried and restores to the Rhinemaidens the much traveled ring.

All of which shows how a whole trilogy can be hung, like the stage curtain, upon a ring.

There could be nothing simpler, could there?

As may be well imagined, there were a certain number of more or less clever parodies of the Tetralogy, all of which are now quite forgotten. We may cite as examples *Rhinegold-Keingold,* "Gold of the Rhine that is no Gold at all," a parody given in 1869 at the Theater of Marionettes at Munich; *Der Tiefe Trunk zu Schweigelsheim oder die Walküren,* "The deep Dive at Schweigelsheim or the Walkyries," a grand opera performed by the Society of Artists at Vienna, in 1876 and 1879; *100,000 Florins und meine Tochter,* "A hundred thousand Florins and my Daughter," a farce at the Josephstadttheater; and in 1881

# A GOSPEL IN MUSIC 185

two other parodies of the *Ring,* given in Berlin.

In the *Ring of the Nibelung* we witnessed the redemption of the universe through the restitution of the accursed gold to the Daughters of the Rhine. In *Parsifal,* a profoundly religious work, in spite of the fact that Wagner adhered to no special sect in writing this artistic and metaphysical confession of faith, we are initiated into the redemption of the world through a "guileless fool."

Amfortas, king of the Grail, has fallen into the snares of the magician, Klingsor. He has yielded to the charms of Kundry, the temptress, infernal and divine, slave of evil and servant of good. During his sleep, Klingsor has struck him with the sacred spear, and the wound bleeds ceaselessly. Who will atone for the sin?

A young and surly lad approaches. The instinct of nature possesses him at first, as it did Siegfried. He wounds a swan, but at the sight of the blood he learns to feel pity. This guileless fool is destined to be the conqueror of Klingsor.

In spite of his innocence, we see him protecting himself against the exquisite and dangerous sorceries of the Flower-Women. The enchantress Kundry, who is in league with Klingsor, succeeds only in inspiring him with a hatred for evil. In vanquishing this rose of the inferno he has conquered desire, has torn aside the veil of illusion, and is ripe for the sacred task of redemption.

And now we see Parsifal on Good Friday, in the valley of Montsalvat. He saves Kundry and baptizes her. It is the hour of the Last Supper. Amfortas is unable to pay the last rites to Titurel, who is dead. Parsifal touches the thigh of Amfortas with the recovered spear. He stands revealed as the Saviour and Kundry dies at his feet. With the return of the kingdom of God upon earth, we have the apotheosis of Wagner's work.

It is worth while in connection with this supreme achievement and one of such rare

## A GOSPEL IN MUSIC

religious intensity, to recall the fact that the Master of Bayreuth dwelt at length, in *My Life,* upon the character of his mother:

"She was," he tells us, "deeply religious. She often preached veritable sermons to us, full of pathos and emotion, in regard to God and the divine element in man. She used to gather the whole family around her bed every morning. She had her coffee-and-milk brought to her, but she never touched it until one of us had read a psalm from the prayer-book."

In precisely the same way that it helps us to explain the philosophical evolution of Kant, if we carefully consider the influence of his pietistic education, so in the case of Wagner we find a curious interest in studying the early impressions of his childhood in regard to religion. His anxiety, his fears and his fervor, following upon periods of indifference, to which he also confesses in *My Life,* through very valuable side-lights upon the religious intensity of *Parsifal:*

"At my confirmation, which took place on

Easter, 1827, the spirit of insubordination revealed itself by the scant respect which the outward forms of the ceremony aroused in me. The child who a few years earlier had cast glances of painful ecstasy at the altar of the Kreutzkirche in Leipzig and formulated a prayer, in his mystical transports, that he might be allowed to be crucified in place of the Redeemer, this same child no longer felt the respect due to the pastor who was conducting the confirmation. He did not hesitate to join in with other lads who were making sport of the minister, and he even went so far as to spend on sweetmeats part of the money intended for the contribution box, in company with a band of young rascals who all met together for the same purpose. Nevertheless, at the moment of my communion I realized my state of mind and was almost terrified by it. While the communicants, of whom I was one, advanced in a procession towards the altar, the organ swelled forth and the voices of the choir soared upward. My emotion as I received the bread and the wine was so intense that it has remained with me unforgettably ever since. It is for this reason that I have never again, from that time onward, partaken of the communion, for I have always feared that I should be unable to experience the same sensations as before. Such a renunciation was possible in my case, because Protestants do not believe that repeated communion is obligatory."

It would undoubtedly be rash to take these passages, or other similar ones, as a basis for any sort of a thesis intended to define the religious convictions of Wagner. Instead of losing ourselves in all sorts of hypotheses, it is best to avoid all formulas, and merely recognize that his mysticism rests upon certain early impressions and harmonizes well with the development of his creative mind. The creator is greater in his art than in his dogmatism.

We must not demand rigorous precision from poets and prophets. It is so pleasant at times to live in the midst of their enchantment and serene radiance. We are quite at liberty later to return to reality and cultivate our garden with much care and prosaic attention.

After having poetically expounded the symbols contained in the mystic drama of *Parsifal*, Catulle Mendès concluded as follows:

"The intellectual life of Richard Wagner attained its zenith in that work of sacred purity and angelic faith. Having attained the highest pinnacles of religious dreams, how could he have descended from them? How could he have returned among men, after having been so near to God? To Richard Wagner's tortured heart, haunted perhaps by repentance for past hatreds, the grace was given that he should die in the midst of prayer."

## CHAPTER IV

THE WAGNERIAN CULT—THOSE FOR AND THOSE AGAINST IT—THE INITIATED AND THE PROFANE—WAGNER IN THE JUDGMENT OF POSTERITY

WAGNER has at last taken a glorious place in the art, the social life, the civilization of France. Although he has not succeeded in effecting a radical and absolute change in contemporary musical drama, and although the enlightened public still has the good taste to be eclectic, no one any longer dreams of denying the bigness of his attempt and the importance of his personality and the part he played in the history of music and the drama.

It would be necessary to review an entire epoch of contemporary history, in order to understand thoroughly the influence of Wagner in France. And how hard it is to be impartial!

But it is not our province to re-try the case, nor to analyze in detail the struggle that lasted for nearly half a century between the Wagnerians and anti-Wagnerians. And, strange as it now seems, this struggle was fierce, violent, even savage. As we read over the criticisms, the attacks and rejoinders, as we acquaint ourselves with all the documents both for and against Wagner, the greater part of which have been carefully collected by M. G. Servier, we find ourselves utterly amazed.

How far off it all seems, almost as far off as the quarrel between the supporters of Gluck and Piccini in the eighteenth century! And yet it was really very close to our day.

We have among us Wagnerians dating from the first hour or the second, hesitating, timorous souls of earlier times who have become converts, former bitter adversaries of the master of Bayreuth, now more or less disarmed by his success, and Wagnerians of yesterday and the day before who deserve no credit whatever for defending a fame that is already consecrated.

All of these indulge in extravagant transports and are as fanatical in their own way as the most rabid adversaries of the German composer are in theirs. They allow no one to touch their idol. Wagner's glory has no need of such excesses of either zeal or insult.

Let us examine the passions which swayed the two parties. All sorts of elements must be considered in studying the history of the introduction of Wagnerian drama into France.

In the first place, we have the morose and intolerant character of Wagner himself, whom his reverses, his unpopularity, his failure to be understood had all tended to embitter. That many people took too literally the proud caprices and mordant aphorisms of a romantic artist of uneven temper, profoundly impulsive and excessively nervous, is undeniable. From the time of his first sojourn in Paris, his misfortunes, according to the opinion of a contemporary, made him "peevish, sullen and insolent."

On the other hand it was certainly not to the interest of the musicians who had already found favor with the public to burn incense before an innovator whose whole thought they could hardly grasp all at once, and who threatened to dethrone them. Such was the case of Meyerbeer, who had already triumphed, and of Berlioz, impatient for a well deserved recognition.

Nor is it astonishing to see Rossini somewhat troubled by Wagner's creed. It is related that the celebrated author of the *Barber of Seville* was as much afraid of journalists as he was of catching cold. He blamed these knights of the pen, hard up for copy, for many an ironic paragraph in connection with the composer of *Tannhäuser,* such, for instance, as the following:

At a certain big dinner, an excellent sauce was served, and the mistress of the house was

## WAGNER AND POSTERITY 195

greatly distressed because the turbot had not been brought in.

"Well," Rossini is reported to have observed, "is not that precisely the trouble with Wagner's music? Good sauce, but no turbot, no melody."

In his *Personal Souvenirs,* M. Michette tells of an interview between Rossini and Wagner, and he adds that, although they did not meet again, they continued to hold each other in high esteem.

Nevertheless, Wagner did not hesitate to ridicule some of the musicians who then enjoyed the highest repute. In his intimate talks with his friends, in the Rue Lord Byron, he said in reference to this same Rossini, that he was filled to overflowing, not with music but with sausage. Auber, on the other hand, impressed him as a true Parisian, brilliant and scintillating.

The music of Halévy's operas was, he held, merely for surface show: "I admired sincerely when I was young," he added, "I was something of a fool, as we are all apt to be at that naïve age."

It is quite true also that Wagner found Halévy himself cold, pretentious and uncongenial.

In Gounod he saw an exalted artist, and a charming conversationalist, but lacking in breadth and depth, and capable only of skimming the surface of these qualities, without really attaining them. To the great poet-musician of *Tristan* Gounod's *Faust* presented only a surface sentimentality, barely skin-deep, "as superficial as a pair of gloves, not to mention rice powder." And Wagner, while humming the "insipid" air of the *Jewel Song,* admitted that Gounod had real talent, but was incapable of rising to the height of certain subjects.

This vivacity which Wagner showed, both in his conversation and in his writings, some of which impress us, not merely as pamphlets but as searching investigations, explain a host of things. And when Wagner proposed simultaneously a new theater and a new worship of the Beautiful, he could not fail to be received with open arms by the initiated, and with hatred by the great majority of the profane.

It was in the middle of the nineteenth century that the name of Wagner began to penetrate into France and to be uttered in artistic circles. Gerard de Nerval, having attended a performance of Lohengrin given at the inauguration of the statue of Herder, made no mistake as to the importance of such a revelation.

"An original and daring talent has revealed itself to Germany, and has so far spoken only its first words."

It was at this epoch that Fetis, with ill considered zeal, denounced Wagner as the enemy of sane traditions, in a libel which Charles Baudelaire openly qualified as "undigested and abominable." Fetis accused the German musician of subordinating music to poetry. What was the course of his system? he asked:

"Because Wagner is without inspiration, because he has no ideas, because he is conscious of his own weakness in this respect, and is trying to hide it."

At the time of Napoleon III's visit to Stuttgart (1857), an opportunity was officially given to the French journalists to hear *Tannhäuser*. Théophile Gautier, great artist that he was, though in point of fact more interested in painting than in music, concluded his criticism in the *Moniteur* in the following terms:

"We should like to see *Tannhäuser* executed in Paris, at the Grand Opéra."

We have already seen under what conditions it was destined to be . . . *executed* a few years later.

Reyer, correspondent for the *Courrier de Paris*, while not assuming the rôle of a neophyte, could not hide his very real enthusiasm:

"I felt electrified," he confessed, "by the magnificent love duet sung by the Knight Tannhäuser and Elizabeth, at the beginning of the second act. And at the end of that act the composer has risen to the most sublime heights of dramatic art."

## WAGNER AND POSTERITY 199

Thus, the two camps were forming little by little. It was not to be long before they would come to blows. Meanwhile the debate remained fairly pacific. His theories were freely discussed. At all events, he was taken under consideration, and fashion paid him a more or less ironic tribute.

Thus, for example, in the *Carnaval des Revues*, an operetta with words by Grangé and Gille, and music by Offenbach, the "composer of the future" was seen to rise from a group of musicians of the past, and end by falling head over heels over the prompter's box into the arms of the perturbed conductor!

M. Servières has collected a good deal of curious testimony from various sources regarding the concerts given by Wagner in Paris. We must at least cite this opinion, by one of the boldest champions of the author of *Lohengrin:*

"Wagner has learned how to be great, eloquent, impassioned, impressive, with the simplest of means; his free and penetrating orchestration fills the auditorium. The attention is not distracted by any individual instrument, they are all harmoniously blended into a single whole."

Hector Berlioz, who was at first regarded as more or less a disciple of Wagner's and who suffered from being so far misunderstood, nevertheless added his tribute of praise to *Lohengrin:*

"It is as smooth and harmonious as it is fine and strong and sonorous. In my opinion it is a masterpiece."

But the music of the future had the faculty of kindling his anger, and seemed to awaken in him a personal resentment. Hence his tone was acrid and full of needless rancor.

Wagner replied this time with great dignity, in a letter which was published in the *Débats*, and in which he expressed astonishment at having been so ill treated by an eminent artist and an intelligent, cultured and sincere critic, whose friendship he himself had valued. He sought for some ground for conciliation and

## WAGNER AND POSTERITY 201

complained in his turn of that ridiculous catch-phrase, "the music of the future."

We need not dwell further at this point on these famous performances of *Tannhäuser* at the Opéra. In his brilliant work on Wagner, Catulle Mendès has characterized them in excellent Wagnerian terms:

"Cries, hisses, howls, boxes rising in revolt, galleries suffocated with laughter behind their fans, orchestra chairs bounding with anger . . .

" 'Where has he come from? Who is this new man who dares to change everything? What, not a single cavatina? We especially want roulades, trills, arias, and other small diversions. And we want ballets, oh! we absolutely insist on ballets!'

"And, augmenting from scene to scene, from act to act, interrupting the performance, disorganizing the orchestra, terrifying the actors, the clamors of the hostile crowd, which had begun to laugh and scream and howl even before the curtain was raised, produced an immense *charivari*, a continual rough-house which could not be drowned out by the searing harmonies of the violins nor by the impassioned cries of the courageous Marie Sasse."

Mendès had good reason for using the word *charivari*. The periodical of that name had been persistent in its attacks, through the press of Pierre Véren and the nimble pencil of Cham, upon Wagner and the "composer of the future."

They extended their attacks to the partizans of this noise-loving composer and cheerfully consigned them all to Charenton; they proposed that the extract of Wagneriate should be substituted for valerianate of potash, and they urgently advised the dentists to replace the customary drugs employed for allaying pain, with music boxes equipped with selections from Wagner!

While Albert Wolff, after a period of indecision, opened a fierce attack against Wagner, and Auber defined him as a Berlioz without poetry and asserted that *Tannhäuser* produced the sensation of reading without drawing breath, a work without punctuation, Prosper Mérimée declared in his *Correspondence:*

"One last disappointment, but a colossal one, was *Tannhäuser*. It seems to me that I could write something very like it tomorrow, by drawing my inspiration from my cat walking up and down the key-board of my piano."

The fiasco of *Tannhäuser* at the Opéra did not fail to evoke a deluge of witticisms at Paris, some more clever than others, but not calculated on the whole to give a very high impression of that type of humor. Is it to be wondered at that such parodies as *Panne aux Airs,* by Clairville and Barbier at the Déjazet Theater, and *Yameinherr* by Thiboust and Delacourt, with music by V. Chéri, at the Variétés, had the short-lived success which they merited?

Oscar Comettant placed himself at the head of Wagner's detractors, in a veritable frenzy that unsparingly included Schumann and Liszt. He proclaimed:

"Wagner thought that he was going to cause

a revolution at the Opéra, but he caused nothing but a riot."

Paul de Saint-Victor talked of musical chaos, and Gozlan blithely insisted that there had not been a musician of such power . . . since Robespierre!

The offended Berlioz continued, as Wagner himself did in only too many cases, to sacrifice justice to his passions, and made the mistake of declaring himself superbly avenged. Scudo also, in the *Revue des Deux Mondes*, made a savage assault upon the innovator.

Wagner was defended, however, by J. Weber in the *Temps*, and by Franck-Marie in the *Patrie*, while in Baudelaire, whose death he deplored later as much as that of Gasperini, he found a clear-minded and eloquent champion. Baudelaire's study of Wagner, which appeared in the *Revue Européenne*, and was afterwards reprinted in *L'Art Romantique*, was a revelation to a great many artists and men of letters.

Another man who showed an admirable constancy and devotion, as well as a fine and disinterested discrimination, was Pasdeloup. In spite of incredulous smiles, disapprobation and storms of hisses, he devoted himself for more than twenty years (1861-1883) to the heavy, complex, redoubtable task of making Wagner known and understood. Thanks to his obscure, but persevering and highly artistic efforts, Pasdeloup successively won a hearing for the *March from Tannhäuser* and the *Overture to the Flying Dutchman*. Little by little, he compelled the attention both of music lovers and of the general public.

It was impossible to dispute the interest of such efforts, and besides, their success seemed in a certain measure to justify them. That is why another musician of considerable merit, Charles Lamoureux, followed in the same path. Without wishing to disparage his zeal, we must recognize that he probably profited largely from the initiative taken by Pasdeloup.

While Lamoureux was winning applause for the *Pilgrims' Chorus from Tannhäuser* and the *Lohengrin Wedding March*, Pasdeloup was making his plans for producing *Rienzi* at the Théâtre Lyrique. It was at this epoch that Catulle Mendès, one of the most ardent propagandists of Wagner and the musical drama, went to Switzerland to pay a visit to the master. Wagner was undoubtedly on the point of triumphing over prejudice, the ignorance of some and the malevolence of others, when the Franco-Prussian war of 1870-1871 broke out.

We have already seen that Wagner's chief preoccupation was to make his work a sort of monument to the German fatherland, and to lay the foundations of a truly national art. As early as 1868 he published an essay in which he formulated his revolutionary theories, enthusiastically, immoderately, exclusively Germanic. Although he did not follow the example of a large number of German musicians, after the defeat of France, and write an ode to the army, a solemn triumphal march for the victors, he did at least make the mistake of writing a stupid and coarse comedy entitled *The Capitulation,* in which, with rather absurd pomposity, he chiefly attacked the Government of National Defense.

There were a good many people who could not forgive Wagner for this attitude, and they chose, with childish acrimony, to hold his music answerable for his capricious temper, and to accuse him of all manner of misdeeds, thus displaying a futile patriotism which caused even Francisque Sarcey to express astonishment, notwithstanding his small sympathy with innovations and mysticism.

Such intolerance was unworthy of the French nation. Mozart's glory is undimmed in France, notwithstanding that he called Frenchmen fools and clowns, and slandered French women who avenged themselves for his insults in no other way than by applauding *Don Juan* and the *Marriage of Figaro,* and listening devoutly to those exquisite masterpieces.

At all events, in spite of his mistakes and narrow-mindedness, in spite of the sometimes lamentable results of his pride and his blind hatred, Richard Wagner could not deceive himself as to the necessity of winning the support of the enlightened public in France. And after all he was capable of being just and reasonable. For instance, he once wrote as follows to Gabriel Monod:

"My productions at Bayreuth have been more fairly and intelligently judged by the French and the English than by the greater part of the German press."

On the other hand, he declared to M. de Fourcaud, editor of the *Gaulois*, in 1879:

"It is true that I am not produced, and for sad and trivial reasons! But let us say no more about it, it is a thing of the past. . . . I am supposed to bear malice, malice! Why should I? Because *Tannhäuser* was hissed? But are they sure that they ever heard *Tannhäuser* as it really is? As for the press, I have not so much to complain of as has been said. I did not pay calls on the critics as I did on Meyerbeer; but Baudelaire, Champfleury and Schuré have none the less written the finest things that have yet been said of my dramas. Even

RICHARD WAGNER'S MONUMENT AT BERLIN
This monument, erected in the Tiergarten in Berlin, by the sculptor Elberlein, is worthy of his universal and colossal glory

## WAGNER AND POSTERITY 209

today the most flattering appreciations come to me from your country. In short, you see that I have no reason to be so dissatisfied as has been claimed. And neither am I."

As may well be imagined, Wagner's ancient adversaries, far from disarming, had mustered up new weapons against him, and found much satisfaction in exerting considerable cleverness and some rather questionable humor in fostering the public antagonism towards the German composer. The bitterest enemies of the author of the Tetralogy were not content to describe him in Tissot's terms, unflattering as the latter's portrait is:

"He has the head of a dragoon: his gestures are as brusque as rapier strokes, and his speech has retained the volubility of a mill-wheel."

Nor did it satisfy their malice to see Wagner depicted in profile, in an ironic caricature, as a hooded falcon, or as a large-headed American woodpecker. They resorted freely to open insults, they denounced the enemy by returning such verdicts as the following:

"Wagner's music reveals the pig rather than the angel."

It is purposeless to cite further amenities of this sort, for they add nothing, and merely demonstrate that music is not always a refiner of manners.

The French composers all suffered, more or less, from this condition of things, regardless of their individual tendencies and their originality. The accusation of Wagnerianism was made, not only against Saint-Saëns and Lalo, but even against Massenet, and at that epoch this was a serious accusation.

Meanwhile, since 1872, Wagner reigned supreme at Bayreuth. Although he was not yet understood as he desired to be, although financial success still remained problematic because of the heavy expenses, although there was ground, and always would be, for discussing theories and systems, it was impossible not to recognize the worth and the splendor of his immense achievement.

Yet, notwithstanding the brilliance of the

## WAGNER AND POSTERITY 211

performances of the *Ring of the Nibelung,* during the summer of 1876, and the ovation which greeted them, they still failed to placate the hostility of certain grim-visaged and stubborn critics from Paris. But there was at least one competent judge among the French envoys, Camille Saint-Saëns, who represented the *Estafette,* and who did not hesitate to express his admiration for Wagner's lofty conceptions, although at the same time he saw no necessity for participating in the full rites of the Wagnerian cult.

At the other extreme, Albert Wolff, of the *Figaro,* continued to indulge in sarcasms that were sadly lacking in philosophy:

"Wagner's poetry," he wrote, "makes most indigestible reading. No one but a man who has trained himself for a week on a diet of American lobster and other notoriously heavy dishes can survive such reading."

Meanwhile, in Paris, M. Pasdeloup, ably seconded by M. A. Jullien, had renewed his generous efforts. Nevertheless, the splendid *Fu-*

*neral March from Siegfried* was hissed at the Cirque d'Hiver, in 1876, the same year in which *Lohengrin* was given at the Théâtre de la Monnaie in Brussels. Admirable side-light on Parisian standards, especially when we remember that the snobbish element gladly accepted *Parsifal* after its almost religious production at Bayreuth in 1882.

On the other hand, while Oscar Comettant still obstinately strove to prove that the Wagnerian drama was a monstrosity, and while even the sudden death of Wagner had failed to suspend hostilities that were so injurious to the real interests of musical art, the *Revue Wagnérienne* gathered together the adepts of doctrines oftentimes abstruse, and celebrated the glory of the master by a sonnet competition, in which the triumphant cadences proved to be . . . the decadent ones of Mallarmé and Verlaine!

It would have been far more profitable to have brought the Parisians into the presence of Wagner's own works seriously performed, but the times were not yet ripe. Carvalho discovered this when, in 1885, he undertook to produce *Lohengrin* at the Opéra Comique, with such chosen interpreters as Talazac and Bouvet, Calvé and Deschamps. It was the signal for a new campaign against Wagner, and more vehement than ever. They even went so far as to accuse him of having tried to set fire to the city!

The Wagnerians, nevertheless, by this time made a good showing and included in their ranks musicians of the highest talent, such as Mme. Holmes, Messrs. Chausson and Chabrier, who passed away all too soon, Gabriel Faure, Messager, and Vincent d'Indy, to all of whom the musical art of France is indebted for numerous reasons; and writers such as Edouard Rod, Maurice Bouchor, Elémir Bourges, etc.

A clever writer on the *Vie Parisienne* has portrayed in the following amusing terms certain significant types among the more fanatical Wagnerites of the fair sex:

"1. *The Eccentric Woman.* She loves Wagner because he is noisy, because he is strange, because he gives us the song of dragon and nightingale, of giants and dwarfs, of flowers and stones, of women on horse-back and women in water, . . . because he endows his heroines with phenomenal virtues and pyramidal vices, because he has hidden his orchestra from view, because the world at large cannot all go to Bayreuth, and because she would find it extraordinarily pleasant to fall asleep, like the Walkyrie, in the midst of flames.

"2. *The Woman of Wealth.* She loves Wagner because it is the correct thing, because she thinks it gives her a special artistic air, because it enables her to transport herself to Bayreuth with a retinue of forty-nine servants, seventy-three horses and a hundred and forty-six trunks, and because she wants to applaud *Lohengrin* in 1885, as a princess applauded *Tannhäuser* in 1861.

"3. *The Up-to-date Woman.* She loves Wagner because it is up-to-date, because it is the latest fashion, because it is a sport like any other, because it is 'deliciously decadent' to go on Sunday '*chez* Lamoureux,' because it is very select to go to Bayreuth, because it gives her a certain stamp of pure cosmopolitanism, . . . and because it is quite becoming to her, decadent flower of the closing century, to sigh as she thinks of young maidens that have stepped straight out of medieval missals."

They have not even yet entirely gone out of circulation, these fair Wagnerites. But it is true that they have for the most part become converts to Debussy.

We know that today Wagner has no difficulty in achieving triumphs at the Opéra, without in any way usurping the place that is due to the French composers. There are Wagnerian seasons both in Europe and in America, and Wagnerian museums at Bayreuth, Eisenach and Vienna.

After the fervent admirers, after the millionaires, æsthetes and snobs, the general public has acquired a taste for these admirable spectacles and cordially applauds them.

*Lohengrin* and *Tannhäuser* now form a part of the classic repertory. We are already far removed from the days of the Wagnerian performances given by Charles Lamoureux at the Eden Theater, and it is twenty years since *Lohengrin*, "opera in three acts and four tableaux, by Richard Wagner, translation by Ch. Nuitter," with a cast including Rose Caron and Fierens, Van Dyck, Renaud and Delmas, took the Parisian public by storm (September 16th, 1891).

Worthily glorified, misunderstood, and reviled, Wagner met in other countries much the same fate as in France. He has not failed to be ridiculed, not only as composer and poet, but also as a jack-of-all-trades and master of universal knowledge. It is in this connection that M. J. Grandcarteret cites quite appropriately an article which appeared about 1882 in the Berlin *Ulk*, under the title of "The Vegetario-Wagnerian Conservatory." It will be seen that the author of *Parsifal* is treated far from reverentially in the course of it:

"Richard Wagner had declared to his followers that a vegetarian diet is indispensable for the reorganization of humanity, that is to say, for the purpose of making it possible to appreciate the works of the Master. It is quite certain that persons habitually nurtured on roast beef, roast goose, partridges and lobster salad will find it impossible to understand even the smallest part of the charm and greatness of *Parsifal*. That is why they have undertaken to build a model establishment in the neighborhood of Bayreuth, for the purpose of producing true 'Wagnerians' in accordance with the formula. According to report, the interior organization of the establishment will be as follows:

"*Four o'clock in the morning.* The pupils will be roused from their light slumbers exempt from all Wagnerianism by the trumpets of *Parsifal*. They will all betake themselves to the so-called 'Dissecting hall,' where they will meet Herr Edmund von Hagen, who will promptly proceed to give them a two-hour address on the philosophico-psychologico-metaphysico-transcendental influence of the 'matutinal call.'

"*Six o'clock*. First repast, an infusion of thistle leaves. This early morning tea will be sweetened by the accompaniment of the *Wedding March from Lohengrin*.

"At six o'clock Herr Albert Heintz will appear and will render the principal leitmotiv. As a mental drill for the pupils, he will each day have twelve leitmotivs performed simultaneously on six pianos. From this chaos of a world of tonalities, the separate motivs should emerge one by one. As these separate motivs are successively recognized, they must be dissected and minutely analyzed; then they must be learned by heart and played until each pupil is able to sing them without a mistake, sometimes forward and sometimes backward, and even in their sleep.

"After four hours of this work, the principal repast will take place. The pupils will enter the refectory in time to the resounding chords of the march from *Tannhäuser* and will bow before the life-sized statue of the Master.

"Then Herr von Hagen will rise and deliver a brief address, lasting one hour, on the subject of Wagner's influence on the question of diet. He will explain that the true Wagnerite should really eat nothing at all, and that each spoonful of soup consumed is prejudicial to the development of true idealo-artistic creations. After this delicate hint not to linger too long at table, he will propose the health of the Master, and the pupils will intone the *Greeting of the People* to Hans Sachs (in the third act of the *Meistersinger*). After which the repast will really begin.

"The menu, as a matter of fact, will consist of only one dish, which however will vary according to the days of the week. Thus, for example, there will sometimes be served sorrel cooked with pickled cabbage and sweet herbs, seasoned with its own broth, or again thistle stalks boiled until tender, or still again renoncules acres served with sauce *Hollandais*

*Volant* (Flying Dutchman sauce). These repasts will be made more satisfying by the performance of selections from Wagnerian works, so that every pupil will leave the table with his appetite thoroughly appeased. After this succulent feast a promenade of at least two hours will be required, in order to counteract any danger of anti-Wagnerian corpulence.

"*From three to four o'clock* water and warm milk will be served in the reading-room. The only intellectual pabulum furnished will be the *Bayreuther Blätter,* the contents of which will be read aloud in its entirety not less than four times. An orchestra, hidden after the Wagnerian manner, will play throughout the reading, in view of the fact that these profoundly philosophical theses cannot be understood without the accompaniment of music.

"Thereafter, a musical tea will be served in the reception room. The pupils will execute favorite selections from the most recent works of the Master, meanwhile partaking of an infusion of camomile or fennel.

*"From eight o'clock until eleven,* reading at sight from the full score; after which all the pupils will throw themselves down on their beds and be gently lulled to sleep by some of the most brilliant selections in the whole Wagnerian repertoire."

So much for Wagner the Vegetarian. Now for Wagner the Anti-vivisectionist. Wagner was a member of the German Anti-vivisection Society. We have noted on several occasions his fondness for animals. When his dog Russ was killed, he was heart-broken and had the beloved animal buried beside the spot reserved for his own tomb, and composed an epitaph for it. Dickens in his country home paid a similar tribute to a favorite bird.

The *Kikeriki* of Vienna had no scruples in attacking the composer through the anti-vivisectionist.

"The illustrious Master," it said, "could lend his valuable aid to the protection of animals from the cruelty inflicted on them, not by publishing pamphlets, but by an entirely different method; all that he needs to do is to play some selections from his operas in front of the buildings devoted to vivisection, and the studies in vivisection will immediately be abandoned (1879)."

Let us borrow once again from M. Grandcarteret's gleanings the following equally sardonic dialogue between two anti-Wagnerians, which appeared in another issue of the *Kikeriki:*

"A marvelous man, that Wagner! I am absolutely captivated by his personal charm."

"You don't say so? What has happened to change you so radically?"

"Your asking me that proves that you are not acquainted with his latest work."

"What do you mean? Is it possible that he has written anything that is free from discords?"

"It is nothing but a series of cries straight from the heart!"

"And by Richard Wagner? Incredible! What is the name of this new opera?"

## WAGNER AND POSTERITY 223

"It isn't an opera, it is a pamphlet against vivisection."

In ways like these, Wagner was singularly ill treated; but on the other hand, he was fortunate in having had a number of biographers of the first rank, whose efforts cannot be too highly praised, no matter from what point of view we look at them; writers such as Adolphe Jullien in France, and elsewhere Glasenapp, Chamberlain and a host of others. At the same time, his personal reputation has had to suffer from certain works of more questionable authority, such as that of the pianist Präger.

But it seems worth while to dwell especially upon one writer who was the most notorious Wagnerian in all Germany,—and who also seems to have been the most notorious anti-Wagnerian. We refer to the celebrated philosopher, Nietzsche. We shall not presume to attempt a definite elucidation of what might be called, if one were choosing a title for a volume on this poet-philosopher, *The Case of Wagner vs. Nietzsche.* We shall not even dream of trying to give any lengthy interpretation of the Apocalyptic visions of the author of *Thus Spake Zarathustra,* nor of involving ourselves in hazy discussions of the question.

But it is interesting to reconstruct with some exactness this singular episode in the history of contemporary art and, we may add, philosophy. Nothing could be more curious, and certainly nothing could be more essential to an understanding of Wagner's mind and to an estimation of his influence.

A profoundly original mind, and an artist of a brilliant and incisive style, haunted by his conception of a regenerated humanity, and by strange and lofty dreams which were destined later to cloud his reason, Friedrich Nietzsche, after pursuing a course of serious philological studies, turned his attention to mythology and to Grecian and pagan antiquity.

As professor in the University of Basel, he had become deeply interested in Wagner's theories and music. In 1869 he paid a visit to

Wagner at Triebschen, in the neighborhood of Lucerne, and expressed his enthusiastic admiration. Wagner received him eagerly, happy and flattered at this attention. For was not Nietzsche in a position to initiate his fellow citizens into the dogmas of the new drama and the new theory of music made concrete in the form of solemn and picturesque spectacles, destined to set the heart of a whole nation to beating?

And later Wagner wrote to Nietzsche:

"Do not fail to come to see me again, and become better acquainted with my ideas. Intercourse with my fellow countrymen has been hitherto of little profit to me." (This phrase is worth noting and contrasting with his exalted love of Germany.) "Come to the rescue of my somewhat shame-faced belief in what, together with Goethe and a few others, I call German liberty. Reveal to the world what true philology is, and aid me in accomplishing the great renaissance."

We shall see, as Théodor de Wyzewa has ably

demonstrated, that a sort of misunderstanding was destined to arise between these two in regard to this same renaissance, and that this misunderstanding was bound to increase, aggravated in Nietzsche's case by the memory of their former friendship and by the cruel anguish of a soul tormented by its efforts to solve the eternal problems of individual and public morality.

*The Birth of Tragedy* was an indirect hymn to Wagner and Wagnerianism (1871). The grateful musician gladly stored it up in his heart, next to his wife, his faithful and fervent protagonist, Lenbach, . . . and his dog.

Nietzsche, who dreamed of the flowering of a vast and sumptuous Germanic paganism, believed that he had found an ally in Wagner. At the start, the Tetralogy impressed him as a fundamentally anti-Christian conception of the universe and of humanity. But the finished drama of the *Ring,* which he derisively insisted upon labeling "opera," impressed him as hopelessly different from the pagan and Dyonisiac drama whose glorious birth in Germany it had been his dream to witness.

As a matter of fact, there could be no greater contrast than that between themes of pity and redemption which Wagner has exalted in the persons of his blameless heroes and the delirium of conquest of the Superman, who has emancipated himself from all compassion and all charity.

When Wagner met Nietzsche again at Sorrento, and when he had read *Man and Superman*, he was able to realize the profundity of their intellectual disagreement. Nevertheless, he sent him the score of *Parsifal*.

Accordingly, Nietzsche at last reached the point of scoffing at his former friend, quite sincerely and very cruelly, recanting his former profession of faith, and qualifying Wagner with the epithet of mountebank and many another equally expressive. But, as we have already noted, he could not rid himself of the spell of *Tristan*, and in spite of his hostility and morbid dislike. he could not restrain himself from shedding tears,—tears of resentment or, more likely, of sentimental and painful regret,—at the mere mention of the name of Richard Wagner.

In *The Case of Wagner* Nietzsche wrote with bitter irony:

"In his works some one always wants to be redeemed, sometimes a little man, and sometimes a little woman."

Another compatriot of Wagner's, Max Nordau, found such aspersions far too tolerant. Protesting against the deification of this artist, he openly called him unbalanced, a graphomaniac with a muddled brain.

"This phenomenon," he said, "has ended by exerting over the great assemblage of contemporary fools a force of attraction incomparably more powerful than all its rivals. The name of this phenomenon is Richard-Wagnerism."

And he declares tempestuously:

"Richard Wagner represents, in himself alone, a greater quantity of degeneracy than all the other degenerates taken together. . . . In his mental constitution as a whole, he shows

## WAGNER AND POSTERITY 229

the delusion of persecution, megalomania and mysticism; in his instincts we find a vague philanthropy, anarchism, and a mania for revolt and contradiction."

And in support of his assertions, Nordau furnishes a number of proofs, the following in particular:

"Wagner surrounds himself with people who are eccentric, if not mad; such as the Princess von Metternich, daughter of Count Sandov, and such as Nietzsche and Ludwig II of Bavaria."

We need not follow this critic upon grounds that are more or less scientific, nor accuse all Wagnerites of cerebral aberration. We may leave him to bear the full responsibility for his diatribe, without for that reason shutting our eyes to the flaws of genius, or to the element of excess in a cult which surely contains quite as much of nobility as it does of puerility and ignorance.

At the same time, Nordau himself concedes that Wagner possesses the talent of a historic painter of the first order! Is it necessary to remark that an appreciation of that sort is scarcely calculated to satisfy the rest of us?

Tolstoy is another who is scarcely more indulgent towards Wagner's works and personality. This need not greatly surprise us. Aside from the fact that the æsthetic judgments of the illustrious Russian novelist are often extremely singular, it is important to bear in mind the nature of his own apostleship and religion. Having returned to a sort of primitive evangelism, he despised all manifestations of sumptuous art, and even of any kind of art which did not bear a direct relation to morality.

The little known pages that he devoted to Wagner's music have been admirably translated into French by M. Halpérine-Kaminsky, and constitute a curious and highly entertaining document. It is well worth while to quote from them at sufficient length to reveal the elements of a doctrine quite as revolutionary as that of the author of the Tetralogy.

"Everything in Wagner is calculated for the

effect; the monsters and the magic fire, and the scenes enacted at the bottom of a river, and the darkness of the auditorium, and the hidden orchestra, and the unheard-of harmonic combinations.

"In short, everything is designed to attract. We are not merely interested in the plot: who will kill, who will be killed, who will marry, who is the father, who is the son, and what will come of it all in the end? Curiosity is also aroused by the relationship between the music and the text: the Rhine rolls its waves; how is that going to be translated by the music? The wicked dwarf enters; how is the music going to describe him? How will the music express courage, fire, apples? How will the leitmotiv of the character on the stage combine with those of the characters and objects of which he speaks? The music, too, is attractive in itself: it departs from all the hitherto accepted laws of harmony, and runs into modulations wholly new and unexpected (which is very easy in music so utterly disorganized and unbalanced); the discords also are new; and all this is interesting.

"All these things, poetic rubbish, beauty, effect and interest, all these methods, carried to perfection in Wagner's works, take the spectator by siege and hypnotize him; he is in the condition of a man who has been listening for hours to the delirious dream of a madman, delivered with supreme oratorical ability.

"People will tell me, 'You cannot judge of the works of Wagner, because you have not seen them produced at Bayreuth, in a darkened auditorium, with the orchestra hidden, and with an execution perfected in all its details.' Well, I should answer, there is precisely the proof that it is not a question of art, but clearly of hypnotism. Plunge yourself in darkness for four days, submit your brain to the action of sounds having the most intensely irritating effect on the auditory nerves, and you will certainly arrive at an abnormal state in which you will be ready to applaud enthusiastically any sort of folly. As for that, four days is too much; the five hours' duration of one day of the *Ring*, as I saw it in Moscow, is sufficient; even one hour is enough for those who have no clear idea of real art, and who are persuaded in advance that they are going to see something wonderful, and that to show indifference or hostility would be to acknowledge themselves uncultured.

"I carefully studied the audience at the performance I attended. The men who took the lead and gave the others their cue were either hypnotized in advance, or else quickly fell back into a hypnotic state with which they were already familiar. These hypnotized people were in a state of complete pathological ecstasy. Furthermore, all the art critics,—a class incapable of any artistic emotion, and consequently won over in advance to any work which, like Wagner's operas, is purely cerebral, —also approved with an air of importance, of a work which furnished them with such fine material for a dissertation. These two categories of melomaniacs drew in their wake the city crowd, with the millionaires and the Mæcenases at their head, who, like badly trained hounds, run with the pack that barks the loudest.

"And if there are some who feel outraged at so much absurdity and falsehood, they keep silent, just as men in full possession of their senses keep silent in a crowd of drunkards.

"And thus it happens that a work which is false, coarse and absurd, having nothing whatever in common with art, makes the circuit of the globe, costs millions to stage, and constantly corrupts more and more the good taste of the higher classes, and their appreciation of artistic beauty."

What virulence! What cruelty! Would it not almost seem as though we were listening to a Rousseau who had made himself responsible for modern opera, and was launching the vials of his wrath against the theater? The prophet of Jasnaia Poliana has been unsparing in his denunciation of the prophet of Bayreuth. Let us, for our part, avoid taking sides in this

## WAGNER AND POSTERITY 235

conflict of doctrines. Since we have the good fortune to be able to read *Peace and War* and *Resurrection,* and also to applaud *Lohengrin* and the *Götterdämmerung,* let us guard with jealous care the precious possession of our elective tastes.

The most eminent musicians of France are all in accord to render his due to the German composer and to recognize the unique importance of his personality and his wide influence on the history of the art. Does this mean that after Wagner there will be no further occasion to admire other initiatives and talents of another order? Not by any means.

M. Alfred Bruneau has proved this by example as well as by precept. Apart from all prejudice, he has devoted one of the best pages he ever wrote to the subject of Wagner's influence upon music. We may listen to him not only as one of the best informed of critics, but also as the distinguished author of a number of masterpieces. At the time of the fiasco of *Tannhäuser* in 1861, Wagnerianism had already taken deep root in the soil of France. Here is what Alfred Bruneau says:

"By persecuting the creator of such an art, they deified him, they changed that art which there was nothing to prevent people from discussing, into an unassailable religion, to which, little by little, the whole world became converted, some through calm and clear-sighted reasoning, others through blind and enthusiastic snobbishness. And the adversaries of progress and beauty forged upon the anvil of their own stupidity and disloyalty the solid and avenging weapon which was destined to slay them.

"By uniting the most daring and at the same time most self-assured innovation with the noble tradition of Gluck and Beethoven, a tradition shamefully misunderstood by the Italians of the decadence, and their innumerable imitators, Richard Wagner splendidly and gloriously substituted logic for incoherence, truth for falsehood, poetry for platitude, melody for the couplet, singing for vocal gymnas-

## WAGNER AND POSTERITY 237

tics, inspiration for formulas, the orchestra for the guitar, wealth for poverty, life for death. The disciples whom, with such tendencies, he was inevitably bound to have, naturally flocked to him in proportion as his detractors multiplied."

This could not have been better said. And M. Bruneau goes on to analyze with extreme subtlety the reasons for the influence exerted by Wagner, its advantages and its dangers:

"Our public was suddenly taken by storm by the very works which were formerly execrated and which finally forced open the doors of our theaters. There ensued a mad craze unparalleled in the history of music. . . . Some of our composers, dazzled by the prodigious sumptuousness of such conceptions, entered upon an extremely perilous path, and very nearly lost their way and perished. Through constantly worshiping the sovereign master, harkening to his lessons, analyzing his methods, they unconsciously and with the best intention in the world, caricature him. From that moment, his influence ceases to be good."

M. Bruneau adds that this influence, all things considered, is on the wane. He very justly remarks, to speak only of conditions outside of France, that the composers who are recognized as the heads of the younger schools, such as Richard Strauss in Germany, Puccini in Italy, and Rimsky-Korsakoff in Russia, content themselves with borrowing from Wagner only such elements as will serve for the free development of their thoughts. And the celebrated composer of the *Dream* eloquently concludes:

"Those who saw in the art of Richard Wagner a limit to the efforts of the universe, a definitive achievement, blundered in as clumsy a fashion as those who denied the colossal grandeur, the absolute necessity of that art. A radiant star has warmed and regenerated us, and has kindled in our hearts the flame of love and gladness; he has fertilized the vast field of ideas with the seed of future harvests. No one will ever succeed in banishing Wagner from

# WAGNER AND POSTERITY 239

the place he occupies in immortality, between Bach and Weber."

We subscribe readily to this judgment, which we may supplement with the opinion of M. D. C. Planchet, who is considered by competent judges as one of the composers best entitled to be regarded as leaders of the modern school in France:

"It is certain, and indeed has become almost a commonplace, that Richard Wagner has transformed musical drama. His influence has been felt, in varying degrees, by all the composers who have succeeded him, by those whose temperaments were the most refractory, and even, in a less direct way, by the latest comers, notwithstanding that they claimed to represent a reaction against his tyrannical domination. This influence was exercised not only upon the form of lyric drama, but even upon the very thoughts of his contemporaries and upon their musical expression. This is why we meet with it in all the different forms of the art which have engaged the activity of modern composers.

"It is true that the melody, the Wagnerian phrase has none of those characteristic formulas which are like a sign manual in Mendelssohn, or Gounod or César Franck. It is chiefly by its movement that we identify it, by the accent, and the expression, which at one and the same time is very delicate and very intense. It is through this quality that it has exerted an influence on all contemporary lyric music, broadening and revivifying it. Wagner's music progressively enriched itself through all the special traits of his immediate predecessors, Weber, Chopin, Liszt, and Schumann, whom he assimilated, and blended into a musical utterance possessed of a richness, a liberty, an audacity and an unexpectedness that do not suffice in themselves, but which in his hands are the necessary and varied expression of sentiments and passions.

"Nor has his influence been any less apparent on instrumentation. It is not precisely in picturesque details that his innovations lie, nor in agreeable blendings of tonal values.

## WAGNER AND POSTERITY 241

From this point of view, Berlioz and Liszt are both his superiors, and what is more, they preceded him. What is peculiarly his own is his full and crowded orchestration, that surrounds the action, bathes it, penetrates it, as it were, with a sonorous atmosphere, through which the lives of the characters seem to be enriched and amplified with all the attributes of universal life.

"Finally, there are certain scenes in the Tetralogy, in *Tristan* and *Parsifal*, possessed of such ingenuity, such amplitude and audacity of conception that they have opened up new horizons, even in the domain of pure music.

"I believe that now we have at last freed ourselves, perhaps through the influence of Russian music, but chiefly thanks to our own national temperament, from whatever was excessive and at the same time transitory in such a dominant force. But we have assimilated from Wagner all that is capable of assimilation by humanity as a whole, all that is stimulating and productive and that now forms part of ourselves, part of our own artistic existence."

Let us record further the appreciation of the tenor, Van Dyck; that admirable Wagnerian interpreter who has successively and magnificently rendered Tannhäuser, Lohengrin, Siegmund, Loge and Parsifal:

"Wagner," he said, "has developed and ennobled his interpreters. The gesture illustrates the melody, the word commands the gesture. Any conventional attitude henceforward is repellent and impossible. We no longer have before us a tenor, a basso, a soprano, mezzo-soprano or contralto,—immutable classification of types!—but personages whose task it is to live the story, and who are obliged to be, neither more nor less than the stage setting which frames them, or the orchestra whose symphonies illustrate and accompany it, the interpreters of a dramatic action, and not merely singers giving a concert in costume."

This is precious testimony, which sums up the rôle of Richard Wagner in the history of musical tragedy.

Wagner, the great romantic artist, the great creator of the musical drama, appears as an imposing and seductive genius, quite regardless of what may be the past and the future of Wagnerianism, or the value of his system and æsthetic conceptions.

It is not easy to escape from the influence of such a personality. He was a religious man. He was great not merely because with one gigantic effort he opened a new and fertile era for music, and presided from the full height of his immense and synthetic genius over the evolution of an art, but because he believed that art was religion. He believed that he had not the right to separate the one from the other. He responded with his ringing and prophetic voice to all the voices of nature. He brought to light the mystery whose secret and deep hidden existence we felt within and around us. He intoned the immortal hosannah of Man to the Supreme and Universal. He evoked from the misty darkness of earth some glimpses of a celestial radiance.

**THE END**

www.ingramcontent.com/pod-product-compliance
Lightning Source LLC
Chambersburg PA
CBHW010741170426
43193CB00018BA/2910